A Gathering Of Spirit

A Gathering Of Spirit

A Collection by
North American Indian Women

Edited by Beth Brant
(*Degonwadonti*)

The
Women's
Press

Originally published by Sinister Wisdom Books (1984) and Firebrand Books (1988) in the United States, this edition of *A Gathering Of Spirit* is published by The Women's Press, 229 College Street, #204, Toronto, Ontario M5T 1R4

Cover art by Charleen Touchette
Cover design by Christine Higdon

Canadian Cataloguing in Publication Data

A Gathering of spirit

3rd ed.

Bibliography: p.
ISBN 0-88961-135-1

1. American literature - Indian authors. 2. American
literature - Women authors. 3. American literature -
20th century. 4. Indians of North America - Women -
Literary collections. 5. Canadian literature (English) -
Indian authors.* 6. Canadian literature (English) -
Women authors.* I. Brant, Beth, 1941-   .

PS508.I5G38   1988   810'.8'09287   C88-095383-7

Acknowledgments

The existence of this issue owes much to the following people:

Michelle Cliff and Adrienne Rich . . . for embracing my idea of an issue devoted to North American Indian women's writing and art. For helping me give it fruit. For not interfering. For friendship.

Paula Gunn Allen . . . for her enthusiasm. For giving me names, addresses. For her good talk.

Brother Benet, Peter Blue Cloud, Carol and Joe Bruchac, Larry Evers, Geary Hobson, and Maurice Kenny . . . for their support and sharing of resources.

Terri Meyette and Mary Moran . . . for giving me sisterhood when I needed it most, often at personal risk. For sharing hope.

Janice Gould . . . for her music. For her bravery.

Jenny Collins of *Madness Network News* . . . for telling me the story of Saralinda Grimes.

Janet Grimes . . . for sharing memories. For her feminism.

Gloria Anzaldúa . . . for two weeks in Santa Cruz at Women's Voices; teaching me, through her example, what being an editor means—seeing with the heart.

Denise Dorsz . . . loving partner. Who had faith. Who listened to ideas, rages, tears. Who was solid and always there.

To the Indian women in prison . . . who wrote me countless letters, and told me their stories; who trusted me. The words—strong, resisting, surviving—seem inadequate to describe lives that most of us can only imagine.

To every Indian woman who wrote, who sent in her work, who enriched my life with incredible images and language. Who gave spirit, who gave a past *and* a future. **Kunorúhkwa.**

Contents

A Gathering of Spirit

I want to write about what it means to put together an issue by North American Indian women. I need to explain and share my feelings connected to that work. There is an urgency to relate the physical details, the spiritual labor, the ritual, the gathering, the making. Because in the unraveling, the threads become more apparent, each one with its distinct color and texture. And as I unravel, I also weave. I am the storyteller and the story.

————

Jan. 3, 1982—Montague, Massachusetts. I am visiting Michelle Cliff and Adrienne Rich, editors of *Sinister Wisdom*. We are sitting in their living room. Dinner is over. It has been snowing all day, the white flakes muffle any sound coming from outside. Michelle has lit the oil lamps. The light is warm yellow and soft. We are talking about writing. About women of color writing. I ask if they had ever thought of doing an issue devoted to the writing of Indian women. They are enthusiastic, ask *me* if I would edit such a collection. There is a panic in my gut. I am not an "established" writer. (To this day, I am not sure what those words mean.) I have never edited any work but my own. And I do not have the education. And to me, that says it all. To have less than a high-school diploma is not to presume. About anything.

I don't say these things out loud, only to myself. But I do say polite words—I'm sure someone else could do a better job, I really don't think I have the time, etc., etc.

Michelle assures me that editing is not the mysterious process I think it is. Adrienne tells me that they would not consider undertaking such a project. One is Black. One is Jewish. Neither is Indian. So I am caught, asking the *inside me*, why did I raise this if I wasn't willing to take it on?

As I lay in bed that night, I wrestle with this very complicated question. And I struggle with the complicated realities of my life. I am uneducated, a half-breed, a *light-skinned* half-breed, a lesbian, a feminist, an economically poor woman. Can these realities be accommodated by my sisters? By the women I expect to reach? Can I accommodate their realities? I think about responsibility, about tradition, about love. The passionate, stomach-tightening kind of love I feel for my aunts, my cousins, my sister, my grandmother, my father. And so, I am told—it is time to take it on.

THE PHYSICAL

I have a two-page list of names, the Native American Directory, and my own list of correspondence. I buy a roll of stamps. I begin sending out the flyer that took me weeks to write. Did it say enough? Did it say too much? Always the questions. I buy another roll of stamps. Send out the flyer to Indian newspapers, journals, associations, organizations, for I know that what I am looking for will not be gotten from feminist or lesbian/feminist sources. I write personal letters requesting support and help in this important project. I buy yet another roll of stamps, more envelopes, have to get more flyers printed. And the fact is, if *Sinister Wisdom* were not paying for these endless stamps, xeroxing, printing, etc., this would be impossible for me to do.

I wrote everywhere I thought there was a story to tell. I wanted to hear from the women yet unheard. I wanted the voices traditionally silenced to be a part of this collection. So I wrote to prison organizations in the U.S. and Canada. I made contact with the anti-psychiatry network, Native women's health projects. I sent to everyone I could possibly think of and then looked for more. Some women requested flyers of their own to distribute among their friends, their relatives, their workmates. To these women I am indebted. Because they took us seriously. Because they had faith.

After a while it became impossible to keep track of how many letters and flyers were going out. My life from June 1982 to February 1983 seems a flurry of typing, going to the post office, going to the printer, making phone calls, writing more letters. I felt I was heading off something. My own writing suffered. My life became measured by *The Issue*. It had taken over. It had become my work.

As the first letters and poems and stories and photographs came to me, I had to reassess, once again, who it is that we are. And why I was doing this. The answers seemed obvious, but were knotted together in a pattern not quite recognizable. I am doing this because I have to. I am doing this because no one else will do it. I am doing this because it is my work. But there was more. It would come when I was ready.

THE SPIRITUAL

"Dear Beth,

Please help me find out who I am. My mother was Indian, but we were taken from her and put in foster homes. They were white and didn't want to tell us about our mother. I have a name and maybe a place of birth. Do you think you can help me? I always wanted a sister."

9

"Dear Sister,
These poems might not be what you are looking for, but I send them anyway. I never wrote before, but wanted to share my memories of my grandma with you. My spelling is not so good, but maybe you could clean it up."

"Sehkon,
How good it is that you are doing this for Indian women. Please accept this story in the spirit I give it to you. I am glad a sister is doing this work."

"Dear Beth,
I am in prison. It is hard to be an Indian woman here. But I think about the res, and my father and mother. When I get the loneliest, my grandma comes to visit me. It is very strange to be away from the land. A part of me stays out there with the birds. Please write to me."

Sister. The word comes easily to most of us. Sisterhood. What holds us to that word is our commonness as Indians—as women. We come from different Nations. Our stories are not the same. Our dress is not the same. Our color is not the same. *Yet, we are the same.* Can I tell you how lonely I have been for you? That my search for the spirit had to begin with you?

The letters. The poetry. Telling the stories. Drawing the pictures. As each day begins, there is new language and image sitting in my mailbox. But it is old too. And as I sort through and sift over the words, it becomes clearer to me. *The power of spirit.* Spirit manifested in the land we walk on, the food that faithfully grows out of that dirt. The wool that comes from the sheep we have raised and sheared. The spinning of that wool into cloth for our families, for ourselves. The story that hasn't changed for hundreds, maybe thousands of years. The retelling. The continuity of spirit. We believe in that. We believe in community in its most basic form. We recognize each other. Visible spirit.

I light a candle that has a picture of the Lady of Guadalupe etched on the glass. I do not light the candle because I'm a christian, but because she is an Indian.

On my bulletin board is a holy card of Kateri Tekakwitha. "Bless me Kateri," not because I believe in the racist and misogynist vision of the Blackrobes, but because she is an Indian.

I want to talk about blessings, and endurance, and facing the machine. The everyday shit. The everyday joy. We make no excuses for the way we are, the way we live, the way we paint and write. We are not "stoic" and "noble," we are strong-willed and resisting.

We have a spirit of rage. We are angry women. Angry at white men and their perversions. Their excessive greed and abuse of the earth, sky, and water. Their techno-christian approach to anything that lives, including our children, our people.

We are angry at Indian men for their refusals of us. For their limited vision of what constitutes a strong Nation. We are angry at a so-called "women's movement" that always seems to forget we exist. Except in romantic fantasies of earth mother, or equally romantic and dangerous fantasies about Indian-woman-as victim. Women lament our *lack* of participation in feminist events, yet we are either referred to as *et ceteras* in the naming of women of color, or simply not referred to at all. *We are not victims.* We are organizers, we are freedom fighters, we are feminists, we are healers. This is not anything new. For centuries it has been so.

There is not one of us who has not been touched by the life-destroying effects of alcohol. We have lost our mothers, an uncle, barely knew a father. We have lost our children. We have lost stories. Our spirit holds loss, held in the center, tightly. We never have to remind ourselves of what has come down. It is an instinct, like smelling autumn, or shaking pollen.

And the core, the pivot, is love. We love with passion and sensuality. We love— with humor—our lovers, our relations, our tricksters. We have a great fondness for laughter. And we do lots of it. Loud, gutsy noises that fill up empty spaces. We laugh at the strange behavior of *wasicu*, we laugh about being Indians. Our spirit is making a little bit of Indian country wherever we travel or live. In cities with the confusing limitations. In universities, where the customs and language are so removed from ours. On the res, where time is often measured by how long it will be safe to drink the water.

I light my candle again. I think of the Lady and her magic. Magic that was *almost* whitened and christianized beyond recognition. Her magic of being a woman, being Indio. Kateri's holy card depicts a white-looking girl, piously praying for the redemption of her people's souls. *But you are familiar to me.* You were dark seers of the future. You were scarred visitations. Beautiful and horrible. *You are us.* Ladies, you frightened them. Sisters, you give nurturance to me.

We made the fires. We are the fire-tenders. We are the ones who do not allow anyone to speak for us *but* us.

Spirit. Sisterhood. No longer can the two be separated.

THE RITUAL, THE GATHERING, THE MAKING

> *"This land is the house we have*
> *always lived in.*
> *The women,*
> *their bones are holding up the earth."*
> — Linda Hogan

"I write on the inside of trees."
— Gloria Anzaldúa

February 4, 1983—Detroit. It does not end here. It begins. It comes down to this. I believe in each and every Indian woman whose words and pictures lie between the pages of this magazine. We are here. Ages twenty-one to sixty-five. Lesbian and heterosexual. Representing forty Nations. We live in the four directions of the wind. Yes, we believe together, in our ability to break ground. To turn over the earth. To plant seeds. To feed.

Our hands. Some are dark, some are light.

Some hands are comfortable with a typewriter, with a pen. Some hands have only just begun to touch paper and pencil without fear.

Our hands are used to work. We work in many places: prisons, universities, cultural centers. As secretaries, as midwives, factory-workers, mothers. Our hands are not smooth.

Our hands are strong. We make baskets, lift heavy machinery, bead earrings, soothe our lovers—female and male, hold our elders. We braid our hair.

These hands fight back. The police, a battering husband, white men who would rape us and the land we live on. We use our fists, our pens, our paints, our cameras. We drive the trucks to the demonstrations, we tie the sashes of our children, dancing for the first time in the circle of the drum. We weave the blankets. We keep *us* a culture.

Our hands live and work in the present, while pulling on the past. It is impossible for us to not do both.

Our hands make a future.

We receive and send back. Our energy and voice reworking spirit. Our woman blood, our Indian blood, churning; refusing to be stilled. *We* have taken it on. All of us.

Beth Brant
Detroit, 1983

May 1984

"Dear Beth,
You will never know how much this book means to me. *It is real. It is the truth.*"

"Beth,
I have learned about courage, about pride, about survival. Indian women have given of ourselves with love and hope. May we continue to learn from each other."

"Sister,
To see my name in print for the first time is like giving birth. I feel new. To have *our* very own book, the first of its kind, is like seeing the sun. We shine, give warmth, and make things grow. Our struggle is so much easier, knowing we have each other."

I have received hundreds of letters like these since *A Gathering of Spirit* was first published. And each one has made me cry. Tears that come from that particular kind of soul-joy in knowing that *we have been heard,* and that our voice is multiplying in strength and coming back in different tongues.

In less than one year, 5,000 copies of this book have been sold. It has become a text in Native Studies, Women's Studies in Canada and the U.S. Portions have been published in West Germany, Great Britain, New Zealand, Denmark, Nicaragua, and Australia. It sits proudly on the shelves of libraries in Indian schools, Native community colleges, Indian centers, shelters for battered Indian women, substance abuse centers, public libraries, the cells of Indian men and women in prison, and in the homes of those who wanted to hear what we have to say. It has been transcribed on tape for the visually handicapped, a sister in Oklahoma has translated several poems and stories into Braille for her blind high school students. Indian newspapers, feminist anthologies, Third World journals have reprinted stories, poems, and essays.

I have personally met and spent time with many of the contributors. Talked and gossiped endlessly on the phone with many. Become dear friends with many. My correspondence with Indian women and men in prison has increased tremendously.

We started something, sisters. Our testament is out there now, part of the wind, part of people's minds and hearts. *We have always been here. We will always be here.*

I thank the people who have written to me, people who are Indian, Black, Asian, Latino, and white.

13

I thank Melanie Kaye/Kantrowitz for the commitment to keep *A Gathering of Spirit* in print.

I thank Indian people, for giving me who I am.

I thank all the contributors. I am inspired by you. I love you.

We *did* take it on, all of us. Truth-speakers, faith-bearers, spirit-givers. We survive in beauty.

October 1988

And our beauty survives through another transition. This Firebrand edition is the evidence.

A Gathering Of Spirit continues to shape and direct what I think, what I feel, what I know. The women in this book have challenged non-Indian attitudes about Indian women. We have inspired new attitudes among Indian people. We gathered our spirit and called it faith. We gathered our spirit and called it love and hope. We are a community. We are a nation. We are alive. We gather the spirit every day—giving it our own names, in our own languages.

I wish to thank Nancy Bereano for giving this book another chance to live in the world.

I wish to thank Charleen Touchette for the beautiful artwork that graces this new cover.

Most of all, I thank Denise Dorsz. She gave me her self—and in doing so, I found my self.

THE MOTHER OF US ALL

Edith Purevich

Artifact

An artifact,
The shards of things
Their hands have held
And used
And laid aside
Remains.
I touch a fragment of their days.

Amber Coverdale Sumrall

Owl Woman

Fire wings soar into forest depths
glazed with moonspill
there are no illusions here
fogwebs hide the source of magic.
Listen to the silence
as it echoes around you,
ancient spirits dance in it.
Take heed
guard your secrets
bury your treasures well,
your knives, your crystals,
your feathers and shells . . .
All your sacred things.
Like ancestors bones
they will be stolen,
pulverized into
instant powder to feed
white men's souls.

Paula Gunn Allen

The One Who Skins Cats

She never liked to stay or live where she could not see the mountains, for them she called home. For the unseen spirit dwelt in the hills, and a swift running creek could preach a better sermon for her than any mortal could have done. Every morning she thanked the spirits for a new day.

She worshipped the white flowers that grew at the snowline on the sides of the tall mountains. She sometimes believed, she said, that they were the spirits of little children who had gone away but who returned every spring to gladden the pathway of those now living.

I was only a boy then but those words sank deep down in my soul. I believed them then, and I believe now that if there is a hereafter, the good Indian's name will be on the right side of the ledger. Sacajawea is gone—but she will never be forgotten.

—Tom Rivington

1.

Sacagawea, Bird Woman

Bird Woman they call me
for I am like the wind.
I am legend. I am history.
I come and I go. My tracks
are washed away in certain places.
I am Chief Woman, Porivo. I brought
the Sundance to my people—I am
grandmother of the Sun.
I am the one who wanders, the one
who speaks, the one who watches,
the one who does not wait,
the one who teaches, the one who goes
to see, the one who wears a silver
medallion inscribed with the face
of a president. I am the one who
holds my son close within my arms,
the one who marries, the one
who is enslaved, the one who is beaten,
the one who weeps, the one who knows

19

the way, who beckons, who knows
the wilderness. I am the woman
who knows the pass, and where the wild food
waits to be drawn from the mother's breast.
I am the one who meets,
the one who runs away.
I am Slave Woman, Lost Woman, Grass Woman.
Bird Woman. I am Wind Water Woman,
and White Water Woman, and I come
and go as I please. And the club
footed man who shelters me is Goat Man,
is my son, is the one who buried me
in the white cemetery so you would not
forget me. He took my worth to his grave
for the spirit people to eat.
I am Many Tongue Woman. Sacred Wind Woman,
Bird Woman. I am mountain pass
and river woman. I am free.
I know many places, many things.
I know enough to hear the voice
in the running water of the creek,
in the wind, in the sweet, tiny flowers.

2.

Porivo, Chief Woman

Yeah, sure. Chief Woman. That's
what I was called. Bird Woman.
Among other things. I have had
a lot of names in my time. None
fit me very well, but none was my
true name anyway, so what's the difference?

Those white women who decided I alone
guided the white man's expedition across
the world, what did they know? Indian maid,
they said. Maid. That's me.

But I did pretty good for a maid.
I went wherever I pleased, and
the white man paid the way.
I was worth something then. I still am.
But not what they say.

There's more than one way
to skin a cat. That's what they say,
and it makes me laugh. Imagine me,
Bird Woman, skinning a cat.
I did a lot of skinning in my day.

I lived a hundred years or more
but not long enough to see the day
when those white women, suffragettes,
made me the most famous squaw
in all creation. Me. Snake Woman.
Chief. You know why they did that?
Because they was tired of being nothing
themselves. They wanted to show
how nothing was really something of worth.
And that was me.

The one who unearthed me was a
suffragette. She had Susan B. Anthony
talk about me at a Women's Rights Rally
out in Utah. Utah. I used to go there
sometimes, to see my friends. Susan B.
said I had done a great thing, leading
those men all that ways. Me,
carrying a baby, mostly in my arms
because his cradleboard was lost—
carried away in a flashflood—almost
took us with it.
Anyway, that's what she said,
and in her romantic way, she was right.
They really couldn't have made it
without me.

Even while I was alive, I was worth something.
I carried the proof of it in my wallet
all those years. They was how I rode the train
all over the place for free. And how I got
food from white folks along the way.
I had papers that said I was Sacagawea,
and a silver medal the president had made for me.

But that's water under the bridge.
I can't complain
even now when so many of my own kind
call me names. Say
I betrayed the Indians
into the white man's hand.
They have a point.
But only one.

One time I went wandering.
That was years after the first trip west,
long after I'd seen the ocean and the whale.
Do you know my people laughed
when I told em about the whale?
Said I lied a lot.
Said I put on airs.
Well, what else should a Bird Woman wear?

But, that time I went wandering out west.
I left St. Louis because my squawman, Charbonneau,
beat me. Whipped me so I couldn't walk.
It wasn't the first time, but that time I left.
Took me two days to get back on my feet
then I walked all the way to Commanche country,
in Oklahoma, Indian Territory. It was then
I married a Commanche man, a real husband,
one I loved. I stayed there nearly 27 years.
I would have stayed there til I died,
but he died first.

After that, I went away.
Left the kids, all but one girl.
She died along the way—not as strong
as she should be, I guess. But
the others—they were Commanches, after all,
and I was—nothing.
Nothing at all.
Free as a bird. That's me.

That time I went all the way
to see the Apaches, the Havasupais,
all sorts of Indians. I wanted
to see how they was faring. I liked
the Apaches, they was good to me.
But I wouldn't stay long. I had fish to fry.
Big ones. Big as the whales
they said I didn't see.

Oh, I probably betrayed some Indians.
But I took care of my own Shoshonis.
That's what a Chief Woman does, anyway.
And the things my Indian people call me now,
they got from the whiteman's words—or
the white women's, I should say.
Because it's them who said
I led the whitemen into wilderness and back,
and they survived the journey with my care.
Its true they came like barbarian hordes
after that, and that the Indian lost our place.
We was losing it, anyway.

I didn't lead em, you know. I just
went along for the ride, and along the way
I learned things a Chief should know.
And because I did my own Snake people survived.
But that's another story.
One I'll tell another time.
This one's about my feathered past,
my silver medallion I used to wear to buy my rides,
to see where the people lived, waiting for
the end of the world.

And what I learned I used. I used every bit
of the whiteman's pride to make sure
my Shoshoni people would survive
in the great survival sweepstakes of the day.
Maybe there was a better way
to skin that cat,
but I used the blade that was put in my hand—
or my claw, I should say.

Anyway, what it all comes down to is this:
the story of Sacagawea, Indian maid,
can be told a lot of different ways.
I can be the guide, the chief.
I can be the traitor, the Snake.
I can be the feathers on the wind.
It's not easy skinning cats
when you're a dead woman.
A small brown bird.

Mary Moran

Thanksgiving Dinner
During Pelting Season (1957)

i.

Two years to maturity. A needle injected into the thigh.
A quick death for the animal with no visible sign of
damage to the skin of the mink.

> After two days of thawing the turkey, she begins
> preparing it. As she removes the soggy wrapping
> of giblets, she wonders if these parts belonged
> to this bird.

An incision in one foot, up the inside of the leg,
round the groin, and down the other leg to the foot.
His hand enters the opening and removes the carcass.

> Rice, chopped apples, spices. She puts the stuffing
> in the hollowed bird and sews it shut. She's grateful
> she didn't have to pluck and gut this one.

The skin is turned inside out and slipped onto a cone-
shaped hanger for cleaning. The hind feet attached at
the top with tacks. The scraping begins. Carefully
the fat is separated from the hide.

> She dips the cotton swab in a small bowl of oil,
> basting the turkey carefully as it turns on the
> rotisserie. The oil burns, the skin browns. Fat
> drips into the pan below.

In the drying room above the feed house, he wipes the hide
with soft cloth. The skins must be bone dry for market.
No oil, no odor.

Her skin is dark like the brown parts of the cooked
turkey. And dry, she says, from the time when her
gas stove exploded when she tried to light it.
The extra fat carried on her small frame came with
marriage and babies.

He smells of mink, of the odor sacs broken. A survival
fluid passed from one species to another. His skin swells
into a softness from another season of mink oil soaked in.
His hair sports the shine of his best pelts.

ii.

Our skin scrubbed clean, my brothers and I sit
at the dinner table with our parents. We're quiet
and still as the mink pelts that hang in the drying
room above the feed house.

"Bless us, oh Lord, for these Thy gifts
which we are about to receive from Thy
bounty, through Christ our Lord. Amen."
She tells us these are the right words,
so we say them. He never says them. He's
not Catholic.

She is French-Canadian and Indian. She denies
the Indian part, so we're not sure whether
our people are Abanaki, Ojibwe, Algonquin, or
Mohawk. When we drive through Shawano on our way
to Escanaba, she tells us the Indians are worse
than the niggers. Worthless drunks, she calls
them and points out the shacks they live in.
You're not Indian, you're Irish Catholic.

The Catholic Church tells us stories about
their early missionaries in Canada. They say
the Iroquois made savage attacks on the clergy.
They say the Indians captured Antony Daniel and
flayed him. They say the Iroquois strung a necklace
of red-hot tomahawks around Jean de Breboeuf's neck,
then "baptised" him in boiling water. They claim
the tribal members drank his blood and that
the chief ate de Breboeuf's heart.

26

He eats the giblets and the neck first, then the dark meat. She prefers the white meat. My brothers want the drumsticks. I don't want any, but take a wing and try to fill my plate with potatoes, vegetables, salad, and bread. She offers us both pumpkin and mincemeat pies for dessert.

Linda Hogan

New Shoes

Even shaking the folds out of the sheet, Sullie formed questions in her head about the shoes. She looked as if she might divine answers from the whiteness of afternoon light in the fine weavings of cotton. The way an old woman might read the future inside a porcelain teacup.

Manny came in quietly, leaving her cart out on the balcony walkway of the motel. "Up where I come from, people read the newspapers instead of the sheets," Manny said, and then she went out the door, her legs two shadows inside her thin skirt.

Sullie tucked the sheets beneath the mattress and smoothed the worn green bedspread across them. It was the color of algae, mossy and faded. New motel guests would arrive soon to sleep between the sheets and the cotton was fragrant with the odor of laundry soap and the smell of scorch from the big mangle. Sullie's short hands tightened a wrinkle away. She watched herself in the dresser mirror as she folded a blanket. Some hair had fallen down the back of her neck. She pinned it up. Her dry and darkened elbows bent toward the ceiling and the pale blue smock rose up away from her hips. She watched the reflection of herself push the soiled bedclothes deep into the canvas bag that hung on the side of the metal cart. In the loneliness of the room, in the mirror with its distortion right at Sullie's forehead and another at her thighs, she saw herself the way others probably saw her, too serious, dark-eyed, her shoulders too heavy, but alive and moving, filling up the room that had never known a permanent tenant.

In the storeroom the black hands of the clock on the wall said 3:00. Already too late for the bus and Donna would be home ahead of her, sitting on the sofa listening for the sound of her mother's shoes, lazily turning the pages of an old magazine. Or perhaps she would have opened the metal wardrobe and stepped into one of Sullie's outdated dresses and stood before the mirror, turning herself this way and that, sticking her chest out a little too far, piling her own dark hair upon her head. With the one tube of dimestore lipstick Sullie bought and once treasured, Donna would paint little smudges on her cheekbones and smooth them out, darken her full lips that were still rosy from childhood. And she would step, barefooted, into the new shoes and stand in the full-length mirror inside the door of the wardrobe and look at the narrow lines of her hips curving out beneath the small of her back.

Sullie unsnapped the blue smock and hung it on the coathook. On its pocket in red thread were embroidered the words, "The Pines Motel." The words hung there in the sky blue cloth like writing from an airplane.

28

"There's only one pine in this entire vicinity," Manny said, "and it's that half-dead straggler over there across the street. Behind the white house."

Manny had already replaced her unused sheets on the shelves, had dropped the canvas bag of soiled linens into the corner for the laundry. "You going to walk?" she asked Sullie. "You ought to take the bus. How much money you figure you save walking those two miles?"

"I only walk in the morning."

"When your feet are still good?" She removed the safety pin from between her teeth and pinned her shirt from the underside. "Does it show?" Manny smiled and the rich gold of her eyes warmed Sullie. Manny with skin the color of earth, black hair straightened only enough to look smooth on the surfaces, like water where the undercurrents twist and pull beneath a seamless and leaden skin. Manny's voice was slow, not full of fast chatter like the other maids, not talking about boy-friends and children, about whether to go dancing or save money for a car.

Manny made thirty-five cents an hour more than Sullie because she was colored instead of Indian. When Sullie got the nerve up to ask the manager about money, he said, "Don't gossip. I don't keep people on when they gossip. And take that chip off your shoulder."

The house with the pine stood alone and surrounded by a few shrubs, a small area of lawn, a remnant of farmland cut through with new streets and clouds of exhaust rising up from buses. In front of the house was a diner and Sullie's bus stop. It was all visible from the second-floor balcony of the motel. The dying tree bent by an invisible wind, shaped like a tired old woman reaching down to touch children.

Sullie seated herself on the bench that advertised used cars.

Manny gestured with her head toward the diner. "Want some coffee?" But Sullie shook her head. "Suit yourself," said Manny, and she walked toward the diner, slowly as if she were wearing green silk and gold bracelets instead of the thin printed shirt and skirt. She went into the diner, a converted house trailer that had an extra room built on the back side of it. The windows were slightly yellow from the grease of cooking. Behind them Sullie could see Manny sliding down into a seat behind the brown oilcloth and the little mustard jar vases with plastic flowers.

Sullie sat outside in the whirl of traffic, thinking of home, of large and slow-moving turtles migrating by the hundreds across the dirt roads, of silent nights when frogs leapt into water and the world came alive with the sounds of their swelling throats.

The wind began to blow off the street. With her hand Sullie covered her face from the dust and grit. Other women held down their skirts, their red and gold hair flying across their faces. A motion caught Sullie's eye. Up in the sky, something white was flying like a large bird. In spite of the blowing sand, she looked up but as she squinted at the sky, the bird lengthened and exposed itself as only a sheet of plastic churning and twisting in the wind. It stretched out like a long white snake and then lost its air current and began falling.

On the bus two elderly women sat in front of her. They were both speaking and neither one listened to the other. They carried on two different conversations the way people did in the city, without silences, without listening. Trying to get it all said before it was too late, before they were interrupted by thoughts. One of the women had steel blue hair. The other one fanned herself with a paper as if it were hot and humid, talking to her own face in the window about her children, one in San Diego in the navy, one in Nevada running a gas station. She put the paper down on her lap and powdered her nose, squinting into the little circle of mirror that was caked pink with powder.

A man with dark hair in front of the women puffed hard on his cigarette. The powdered woman fanned away from the smoke. Sullie watched it rise, nearly blue, into the light of the windows, drifting like a cloud in the air currents, touching the hair oil spot on the glass. It was like mist rising off a lake in the early morning. Steam from a kettle of boiling vegetables, squash, tomato, onion. It smelled good, the sweet odor of burning tobacco.

Buildings blurred past the window. The early shift men carried lunch pails to their cars and buses, all gliding past the window as if Sullie were sitting still and watching a movie, a large fast-moving film of people disappearing into the south. Even those people walking north were swept into it, pulled finally backwards across the window and gone.

Sullie stood and pulled the narrow rope. She felt exposed, the people behind her looking at her tied-back hair with its first strands of white, at her cotton dress wrinkled from sitting on the plastic seat, at the heaviness of her arm, bare and vulnerable reaching upward to ring the bell. She stepped out the door and it hissed shut behind her.

Donna was not there. Her notebook was on the table and there was a dirty glass sitting beside the shiny new dishdrainer Sullie had bought with her last paycheck. Sullie rinsed the glass and placed it, upside down, in the orange plastic drainer, then wiped the glass and the drainer both with a towel. Her shoes creaked the gray linoleum where it was bulging.

Donna's sweater was on the floor beside the sofa bed. Sullie picked it up and then, once again, she reached beneath the sofa and pulled out one of the sleek black shoes. New shoes. They were shiny, unworn. Patent leather with narrow pointed heels and a softly sculptured hole in each toe. Sullie brushed the dust from them with her skirt. She saw her face reflected in the shiny leather, her wide forehead in the roundness of leather. Her heart jumped in her chest again as it had when she first found the shoes.

They were prettier than the shoes Anna May had worn that summer when she came from Tulsa on the back of a man's motorcycle. And Anna May had worn them, dust-ridden, red leather, all the way from the city down the dirt roads, over the big gullies that washed into the soil. She wore them home, wearing also a red and blue dress flying out on the back of a motorcycle.

What a big to-do the family made, admiring the bright dress and shoes even before they welcomed Anna May and her thin-faced boyfriend. Sullie had polished the buckles of her sister's shoes, walked around the floor in the red shoes that were too big and wobbly, her dry and dirty legs rising out of them like old sticks and her ankles turning.

Sullie put Donna's new shoes back under the sofa. She lined them up and put them where they couldn't be seen from the table.

It was dark when Donna returned. Sullie's eyes wandered from Donna's face down the small shoulders held too high, the large hands that were always out of place, looking right down at her feet in the runover saddle shoes. She glanced again at Donna's light-skinned face. "I've been worried," she said.

"I was at a friend's," Donna said.

"Hungry?"

"We ate."

Sullie opened the refrigerator and stood in the light. Steam rolled out the door and surrounded her. She took out the bologna and, sitting at the table, made herself a sandwich.

Donna looked at the window, watching their reflections on the glass. A woman and a girl like themselves sitting in the dark square of glass.

"What did you eat?"

"Meatloaf and potatoes." With her finger Donna traced the pattern of the black matrix in the gold-colored plastic table. "Look, this one is shaped like a hawk. See? There's its wing. See its beak? It's saying, the train is about to come by."

"I haven't had meatloaf in a hundred years," Sullie said. She reached across the table to touch Donna's arm. Donna pulled away, got up and filled the glass with water from the faucet. The water clouded and cleared.

"What do you really think a hawk would say, Mom?"

Sullie was quiet. She stood up and went over to fold the quilt Rena had made. She was careful with the quilt, removing it from the sofa back. Each patch was embroidered with stories of Sullie's life. If Rena had lived long enough, there would have been more stories to stitch, Sullie's life with Donna's father. That would have contained a car and a man smoking cigarettes. There would have been a patch for the birth of Donna, the little light-skinned Indian who would someday wear black patent leather pumps on her bony feet. There would be a square containing the Pines Motel with Sullie standing on the balcony looking out at the yellowing pine tree that had lost most of its needles and looked like an old woman weeping. What else? A small coffin containing her dead son. Sullie taking the bus to Denver with little Donna crying and snuffling next to her. It was all like the great stained glass window, the quilt colors with light behind them. There was a picture for every special event of Sullie's childhood, a picture of Sullie's birth, the swarm of bees, little circles of gold, flying across the pale blue cotton, the old people all standing on the front porch of the old house. One of them, an old woman named Lemon, was wearing a yellow dress and holding the dark infant up to the sun. Her legs were red. There were indigo clouds.

The last patch had never been finished. Rena was working on it the summer she died. On it was the lake with golden fish stitched down across the quilted waves. And there were the two glorious red mules whose backs were outlined in yellow thread as if the sun shone down on them. Men in rafts and boats. A group of women sitting at a table and gossiping were just outlined in ink. Nothing solid to them. Nothing filled in or completed. They were like shadows with white centers.

Sullie folded the quilt and put it on the table beside the couch. "Help me pull out this sofa, will you honey?" She looked at Donna. "You know, I really think the hawk would say, it shall come to pass that all the world will be laid bare by the doings of men."

Donna looked at the quilt. "Can we sleep under it?"

"I'm saving it," Sullie told her once again.

"What for? When you get old and die?"

"No, honey, I just want to keep it nice. When you grow up, I'll give it to you."

Donna lay down between the sheets. Sullie sat next to her and ran her fingers down a loose strand of Donna's hair.

Saving things for old age. The very idea. Sullie reprimanded herself. Saving things when the girl wanted something pretty to hold now and to touch. No good. A mother and daughter alone in the city, no good. It was what happened when you married a man who drove up in the heat of summer after being gone two years and you had to tell him about the death of his son and then you wept and went away with the man, going anywhere just to get out of that desolate place and the heat. Just to get out of that place where your uncle had come drunk and shot his wife, the place where your cousin sold off everything you owned one day just to buy a bottle and then tried to kiss your neck. Not that it was much to look at, but he sold it off to a young couple in a pickup truck that looked like they came from back east. And you went away with the white man and he went into the army. So the hawk would say.

It was better with him gone, with her husband gone. Even trying to earn a living. To mend socks and underwear for only two people. To not have to listen to that man bragging about what he used to be when he sang in bars or when he played baseball with some big team or other. Better to not even get any more of his letters or the snapshots, the shiny snapshots he sent of himself and his army friends sitting it out in bars with pretty oriental women smiling behind him. Still, Donna was growing up different. Like a stranger. She was going to be a white girl. Sullie could already see it in her. In her way of holding tension, of shaking her foot. In the hair she kept cutting. She was growing up with the noise of buses and cars, of GI's and red-dressed women laughing outside the window at night. She wasn't growing in the heat of woodstoves that burned hot even in the summer and the fireflies with their own little lanterns going on and off. Well, she wouldn't be picking cotton for the Woodruffs either, like Sullie had done, feeling mad because Mrs. Woodruff was half Indian herself and spending that cotton money on silk dresses and luncheons at fancy places while Sullie was out there picking it from the dusty fields with her eyes watering. And she wouldn't be growing up laying down with men on the road at night like Anna May had done.

It must have been the quilt that moved her to dream of walking in the big lake at home. The water was warm against her legs. Silent except for the sound of water dripping off her, touching up against the shores in a slow rhythm like maybe it loved the land. And suddenly she was standing in the street by the diner, cars bearing down on her and she was paralyzed, unable to save herself.

Sullie woke up. It was cool. She covered Donna with her own half of the blanket and got up. The sky was growing lighter outside the window, beginning to light up the white cotton curtains with the rose colors of sunrise. Traffic picked up. Standing in her pale gown, her long hair loose and down around her waist, Sullie opened the curtains while the coffee water boiled. She called softly into the other room. And then she went over to pull back the covers. "Time to get up."

Outside, Donna stood at the end of the bench, waiting for the bus. Two young GI's slouched down on the bench. They wore olive drab, one with his military hat pulled down as if he were sleeping, one leg crossed over the other. His hands were folded loosely in his lap. Donna stood almost at attention.

A train passed over. It clattered and thundered along the trestle and it seemed to blow open Donna's tightly held sweater. It blew her hair in a blur of heat and exhaust, the heat waving up like a mirage, a summer field or highway. The soldier who sat straight up waved at an invisible conductor leaning off the platform between cars, and then he glanced at Donna. His eyes took in her thin body and chest. Under his gaze, she was stiff and unmoving. She stared straight ahead, but her body tightened inside her blue-gray sweater.

The train hurried past, carrying coal in the sweating black cars and speeding east on the vibrating track.

Donna was still. In the center of all the motion, the automobiles filled with people, the gold and red plastic streamers that waved and twisted about the used car lot, she was still, and then the train was gone.

Indoors, Sullie wiped the black shoes with a dish towel. She set them down on the table, on the speaking hawk laminated into plastic. She dried the dishdrainer. It was pretty, the color of wildflowers at home. Bright orange like children's new toys and painted Mexican salt shakers, city swingsets. In the morning light, the entire kitchen shone, each item clear and full of its own beauty. The cereal bowls were dragonfly blue. The coffee cup was deep rich brown. It sat on the table beside the black shoes.

The shoes were small. Donna's size. Inside, in the place where Donna's delicate arch would touch and rise when she walked, were the words, "Montgomery Ward." Monkey Wards, as Sullie's cousins called the large white department store on Broadway, the store with the wires going through the ceiling, across the desks, the little tubes of money sliding through air and stopping.

Sullie's own shoes were flat and worn, scuffed. The soles were worn down at the heels. Last week a nail had pushed into the heel of her foot.

Suppose Donna had stolen them, she wondered, standing back and looking at the new shoes. She sipped her coffee. Suppose Donna had stolen these woman shoes? Or stolen Sullie's money. Sullie picked up her handbag and unzipped the money compartment. Eighteen dollars and twenty-nine cents. It was all there.

Sullie imagined the fancy shoes on Donna's little horse legs. With the pink toes and jagged toenails protruding through the sculptured holes. Donna's thin calf muscles flexed above the high heels. Destitute and impoverished thin legs the color of cream and with fine and scraggly hairs and big knees all looking so much worse above the shining black shoes. And there were those young soldiers already looking at the little breasts and at the red-black hair moving unevenly across her shoulder blades. What would they think when they saw the girl walking at a slant, wearing them? Surely they wouldn't want to touch those pitiful small legs and thighs or cup their big hands over the bulges of her breasts.

Someone must have given them to her. The meatloaf friend.

Donna could not count money and she was shy with salesclerks, holding her handful of pennies too close to her own body and waiting for the clerks to reach over and count out what they needed from the moist palm. Donna's schoolteacher, Miss Fiedler, had herself told Sullie that Donna couldn't count money. She had visited their place and all the while Miss Fiedler spoke, her blue eyes darted around the room, never resting on Sullie, who believed the woman was looking for bugs and dust. Those cornflower blue eyes looking at the nailholes in the bare walls, at Donna's drawings taped on the kitchen wall next to the window, at the quilt with its needlework pictures of Sullie and her own mother standing surrounded by a field of green corn with a red turtle floating in the sky like a great sun and a yellow frog and curled scorpion in each corner.

"What's that?" Miss Fiedler pointed at the turtle and the scorpion. "Oh, a red turtle. It looks like it's swimming."

"The sky turtle. From an old story my father used to tell."

Miss Fiedler kept her feet square on the floor and her knees together. Sullie was aware of her own green blouse. It was ironed but growing thin beneath the arms. Sullie remembered to lean forward as she had seen other women do, to look at the teacher's face and occasionally at the pale yellow sweater and its softness and at the blonde curled hair. The teacher sat like a gold light in the center of the sofa that day, like a madonna in a church surrounded by a quilt of stained-glass pictures.

Finally Miss Fiedler looked right at Sullie. "I was passing by and thought I might as well stop in. I thought it would be better than a letter."

"Oh?"

"Donna isn't ready to go on to seventh grade. It's out of the question. She doesn't even count money." She added, "She doesn't get along with the other girls."

And in a long silence following the words, the room brightened as the red turtle sun came out from behind a cloud. The teacher's hair lit up like brass. She expected Sullie to say something. Sullie watched the woman's face brighten. Then she said to the teacher, "She's good at art though, don't you think?" And Sullie went over to open the drawer and remove the collection of pictures she kept there. "See here? This is Lucy Vine. It looks just like her." And there was old Lucy wearing some plants in a sling of cloth on her back. She was bent, nearly white-headed, leaning over a fire. Behind her was a metal tub for washing and some men's shirts hanging along a fence like scarecrows and a raven flying overhead, its blue-black wings spread wide.

"Nice. That is nice."

Sullie looked up at the teacher and repeated, "She's good at art," and the teacher looked back at Sullie and said nothing.

Even remembering this Sullie felt ashamed and her face grew warm. She removed her apron and hung it on the doorknob that was heavy and crystal. The color of larva, with light pouring through it. Sullie lifted the apron and looked again at the doorknob, the room reflected in it a hundred times, herself standing upside down and looking at the tiny replicas of the motel-apartment. She left it uncovered. She put the apron over the back of the kitchen chair. The doorknob was the nicest thing in the room besides the quilt and Donna's pictures. The pictures were lovely. There was one Donna had sketched of Sullie from the back, her shoulders soft and round-looking, the hair unkempt, the heavy face just visible in profile. And there was a picture of women dancing in a row. They wore gathered skirts over their heavy hips, dresses with the sewn patterns, the Diamondback design, the Trail of Tears, the Hand of God. They were joined hand to elbow. Their white aprons were tied in neat bows at the back. "Funny dresses," Donna commented when she completed the picture.

Pretty as a picture postcard, Mrs. Meers was standing at the door with her arms folded, the red and gold streamers flying behind her in the car lot. There were flags on the antenna of a used Chevy that said $250 in white soap on the windshield. Mrs. Meers, the manager, fidgeted with her hair, one arm still crossed in front of her stomach. Sullie opened the door.

"You got a phone call from the motel. They say you're mighty late coming in today."

"The Pines? I'm not going in." Sullie didn't look surprised at the message.

"You don't look sick to me." Mrs. Meers dropped both hands to her hips. They were slim in white pants.

"I didn't say I was sick. Just tell them I'll be there tomorrow."

Mrs. Meers looked more seriously at Sullie. Like a doctor might do when he discovered you were not just entertaining yourself by sitting in his examining room. She squinted and sucked in her cheeks. "I don't mean to step into your business, but to tell the truth I'm not good at lying. You tell them. And tell them to quit calling me. Tell them you'll get your own phone."

Sullie shrugged. "It's not lying." Only the hint of a shrug, so slight that Mrs. Meers did not notice. And she continued talking more softly now. "What's so important that you can't go in? What's worth losing your job over?"

"Look there!" Sullie was pointing toward the street. "Look there. Is that your little cat?"

Mrs. Meers looked impatient. "You know I don't keep cats."

"It'll get run down."

Mrs. Meers tucked in her red shirt. "Look, I know I ain't supposed to be looking out for you tenants."

"Shows through," Sullie said.

"What?"

"Your shirt. It shows through your pants."

The landlady waved her hand in exasperation. "Listen to that. You worry about my shirt."

Sullie half-listened. She nodded. She was still watching the kitten stumble away from the wheels of one car and toward another.

"Okay. Okay, I'll tell them." Mrs. Meers went off grumbling, saying how it was these people could buy fancy black shoes like those there on the table and not ever go to work. Must be government dole or something. She herself could not afford shoes like those and she was running this place. She waved her arm as if to clear her mind, to get rid of Sullie and that sneaky quiet kid of hers. Deserves to lose her job, she mumbled. And all the while Sullie was out there in the street calling to the kitten, a scrawny little cat with greasy fur. "No pets!" Mrs. Meers yelled at Sullie. "No pets allowed. We don't even let goldfish in."

After the cat coiled up on the sofa, Sullie washed her hands and returned her attention to the shoes. If they were stolen, they would have to be taken back. That would be the right thing to do, to hand the shoes to the salesclerk. She might be one of those older, efficient types who wore maroon suits and shirts that tied in bows at the neck. Pearl earrings. Or one of the tall ones in the thin dresses. If she were a young clerk, she would be nervous and call the manager. The managers were tight about the rules. They stuck with the rules. They might call in the police.

Sullie had never stolen anything. Just the thought of it sent her heart racing and made her knees weak. She had no courage against teachers, clerks, police, managers, and even now the fear came flying into her.

She put the shoes back where she found them.

It was a quiet day. Early afternoons were quiet. The traffic died down. The red and gold streamers were lifeless. A good day just for walking.

Sullie stepped across the railroad ties that smelled of creosote and the penny smell of oiled metal. She went across the vacant lot filled with weeds and a few spears of green that were irises. Behind the rows of houses, there was a lake, a few elm trees. She heard the doves in the mornings from her kitchen and she was hungry to look at the water, the blue sky lying down on its surface.

Two ducks swam there. The bright-colored male was showing off. He shook himself, ruffled his feathers and paddled his orange feet. The female ignored him, diving under water with her backside exposed. Dipping and surfacing. A plane flew over and Sullie caught its light on the water.

An old man with a cane tipped his dark hat. He wore a heavy coat as if it were still winter and he had not noticed the change of seasons, the warm sun and the green dusty leaves on the few elms. A woman sat on a swing, her two children pushing at one another. The woman stared at the ducks. Her face looked bored and vacant, the look of mothers with young children. She would have spoken to Sullie if Sullie were thinner and looked different. If Sullie had worn a pair of slacks and a flowered blouse. The woman wanted to speak to someone. She greeted the old man.

When Sullie headed back, she had to wait at the tracks for a train to pass. It was a passenger train and the faces in the windows rushed past. One small boy waved at her. The wheels clattered, metal on metal. A man and woman stood on the platform, the wind in their hair and faces. His arm around her waist. The sounds roared in Sullie's ears and the earth beneath her feet rumbled and shook and then the train grew smaller in the distance, growing lighter and she picked her way over the tracks and through the weeds of the field, out of the heat and cement and into the fresh smell of the grocery store. Cool. The banana odor, the laundry soap fragrance. There were cartons of eggs on the rack, tan and perfectly smooth and oval, red meats with their own fleshy odor. "How much?" she asked, pointing at the ground beef. The man in the white cap gestured to the marker. Sullie ordered a pound and he scooped it out and wrapped it in white butcher paper, wrote .31 on the top with black crayon.

Sullie left the store, walking slowly, her arms full of the large bag, her face to one side of it watching for cracks and settlings in the sidewalk. Carrying milk and a small bag of flour, a half-dozen eggs, an apple for Donna, two potatoes. And there was a small container of cinnamon inside the bag. A gold and green shaker holding in the sweet red odor of other countries, of islands with their own slow women carrying curled brown bark in baskets. The metal box was the color of their dresses, water green and sunlight color.

Sullie would make bread pudding out of it and fill the apartment up with the odors of islands and Mexico, warmth and spice and people dancing in bright colors and with looseness in their hips, at least as far as she imagined.

When Sullie arrived, there was another smell in the apartment, the wax and perfume smell of the lipstick Donna was wearing. The rouged cheeks and red lips made her look younger, against the girl's intentions. Her big dark eyes were innocent in contrast with the crimson lips. The lipstick paled her skin. All of her facial weaknesses were revealed by the rosy cheeks and the painted lips, as if her plainness normally strengthened her, camouflaged the self-consciousness of her expression and the awkwardness of her movements, the pensive bend of her shoulders. She looked away when people spoke to her and she did not look up into Sullie's eyes now while Sullie stood, her arms full of the brown paper bag. She stood one moment before putting the groceries down on the table, and Sullie said, "So." Nothing more or less, simply, "So."

The kitten slept in the child's lap. Its paws were twitching slightly. Down in the quick of it, beneath the smell of transmission fluid, the kitten was dreaming of something pleasant. Cream, perhaps. Or of stalking brilliant green flies. Lord, Lord, Sullie breathed, what things we put in our heads. All of us. Filling ourselves up with hopes. Looking out for an extra dollar or good job. Putting on these faces. Even the cats. And here it was, the kitten, all comfortable while Mrs. Meers over there was plotting how to get rid of it. No pets. All these dreams and hopes, and nothing out there but rules and laws. Even in the churchyards. Even in the big homes, the ones that smell like paint and god-fearing Sunday dinners. Even in the motel rooms, a sign on the door saying when to move on. A bible full of do and don't. A boss clocking you in. Red lights. And there was a girl with red lips whose eyes do not meet yours and her head filled up with pretty things and men who would someday love her right out of her loneliness for a few hours. Her head filled up with pearls, silk dresses, shining hair. Evening in Paris perfume in the pretty blue bottles. All those thoughts flying around in there like crows circling over something down on the road.

Sullie was quiet as she put away the groceries. She removed her shoes and walked on the gray linoleum, her feet with a soft animal sound against the floor. She struck a match against the stove. The odor of sulphur and then of gas as she held it to the little hole inside the dark oven. All at once, as the fire took, there was the sound of burning, of the box-like oven opening up. She was going to cook meatloaf. Donna, holding the kitten, stood by the table and traced the black marbled patterns with her finger. "It's a monkey."

"Does it talk?"

"It says you got fired for missing work today."

Sullie put down a fork. "Who says that?"

"The monkey says Mrs. Meers told him."

"Monkeys lie. Besides, what's he doing hanging around women with black roots in their hair?"

"Did you ever hear of television? It's new. It's like a radio, only with pictures.

And they move like in a movie." She was filled up with amazement and the magic of it. Her eyes darkened. "I saw one."

"How do they get the pictures?"

"They come in the air."

"Pictures? You mean they are in the air?"

"Even in here, and if we could turn on a button they'd show up. Yes, they would." And Donna saw the apartment peopled with men and women, animals, new places, all around her the black and white pictures of the rest of the world.

"I'll be. They think of everything, don't they? They just sit back up there in Washington with old Eisenhower and they think of everything." Sullie rubbed on the soap bar while she spoke and the bubbles foamed up in the dishwater. She smiled down at Donna. She dried her hands. "Sit there. Stay there." She went over to the couch. "Don't move." Donna remained at the table while her mother bent and reached underneath the couch for the shoes. Donna's hands tightened.

"Child," Sullie said, standing up. "I don't know where they come from but they are about your size."

Donna was still. The light from the ceiling was on her hair and behind her, the small lamp burned an outline about her, like a small fire, like a burning match. Her delicate face was soft-looking even with the red lips.

"I found these. Here, put them on."

Donna stood and balanced herself by holding on to Sullie and then to the chair back. She put one small foot inside a shoe and then the other. She stood taller and thinner than before. She looked frail. The leg muscles tightened. She wobbled.

Sullie went to the wardrobe cabinet and opened the door to reveal the picture inside. "Look," she said, and she was almost breathless. "Look. You're pretty."

Donna looked herself up and down. She looked into the depths of the mirror for the moving pictures of men who were flying through ordinary air, for the women selling Halo shampoo on the television. She heard their voices. She looked at the black patent leather shoes. She lifted one foot and polished the shoe against the back of her leg. She stood, turning herself in front of the mirror. Her skin looked moist, childlike in its warmth and lack of pores.

Sullie stood quiet, rocking a little, swaying in place. Donna could see her mother in the back of the mirror behind her, a dark woman, plain and dark and standing way back in the distance with her hair tied, her feet bare, a heaviness in the way she stood there in that air, that very air all the perfect white kitchens floated through, all the starched blonde women drifted into like ghosts. Sullie moved more fully into the mirror, her darkness like a lovely shadow beside the pale girl, her hand on the girl's narrow shoulder.

"Pretty," she said. "You sure look pretty."

Blanket Shawl
painting by Alice Souligny

Diane Glancy

I Am Not the Woman I Am

You are looking at my ghost,
not the woman I am, nor even was
when prairie buckled under black wagons, clammed
shut the grip of plains.
The yellow flowers, the curd of watery faces;
wagons like fish on banks, flopping,
gulping for last breath. Our men watched them
from the hill; we hear the talk of their silvery
breath.
Our broken tribes weep on spirit trails where the man
with a sword in his gizzard and outspread arms
calls us to the prairie's rusted gate.

Terri Meyette

Trading Post – Winslow, Arizona

Momma said I had eyes like a hawk.
Dust, red earthen clay clings
to emerald green velveteen skirts,
flashing opposites
as they quietly sway past a tiny face.
Silver and turquoise slides from a wrinkled wrist,
crosses the counter   to meet its fate
a pawn ticket.
Voices grunt and haggle price,
two bags of flour appear in exchange.
Faces wrinkled and worn
like ancient ruins,
browned like fry bread
parade into the trading post.
Tourists with knobby knees   white socks
and black leather shoes parade out.
Cameras around smog-soaked necks
dead pawn in their white clutches;
they buy history in a blanket,
family traditions in a squash-blossom necklace
the old lady walks home
with two bags of flour.

Debra Swallow

A White Man's Word

The screen door slammed shut, and I just knew eighty flies came in. Then I heard wailing and gibberish and ran to see who it was. My nine-year-old son was running toward me with blood, tears and dirty sweat trickling off his chin, making my knees go weak.

"What happened? Who did this to you?" I asked, kneeling to wipe his round face with a cool, damp cloth.

"I got in a fight, Mom. Mom, what's a half-breed?"

I felt like my blood stopped running, and I closed my eyes to kill my tears, my mind opening up a day I'd almost forgotten.

I opened my eyes to see how under-water looked, and a sting like cactus tips closed them fast. Surfacing, I looked across the pool for my friend. The water shimmered turquoise blue, reflecting nothing but the painted concrete bottom and rectangles of green light from the roof. Forty or fifty pale faces and arms bobbed and floated above the water, but no sign of my friend's brown, familiar face.

"Maybe it's time to go," I thought and swam to the closest edge. Feeling the rough, slimy cement on the palms of my hands, I hauled myself out of the water. Unsure of my footing, I walked slowly toward the shower rooms.

Screams, giggles and little-girl conversation filled the room, along with spraying, splashing and draining water. Stooping to peek under the first shower stall, I saw two white feet and moved on to the second door. Also two white feet. Next door, four white feet. I could feel myself starting to shiver now and my breath felt trapped in my chest. "What if they left me? I don't know anybody here," I thought.

My friend and her mom took me with them to Rushville to swim. My first time alone away from my family, and here I was, scared among white people—the only Indian in sight.

I decided to just kind of stand around in the shower room. I knew she wasn't in the pool, so she had to come here, where our clothes were. Trying to be as un-noticeable as possible, I leaned against a cool, wet wall and watched the white girls in the room, curious because I'd never been around any before.

"My dad bought me a brand-new bike and it has a blue daisy basket on the handlebars," one girl whined to her friend. "Well, I already knew that, but did you know my dad bought me a new bed and it has a canopy on it!" she whined back in a sing-song voice. The two girls were probably eight years old like me, but both were chubby with blonde ringlets and painted toenails.

Spacing out their words, I was thinking about the bike Dad made my sister and me. He made it from all different parts he found at the trash pile, and it looked funny and rusty, but it worked real well. Daddy also made us a pair of stilts, a playhouse and a pogo stick, which all our friends wanted to play with. I knew my dad was better than theirs, he BUILT stuff for us.

I noticed the first girl was dressed now, and while waiting for her friend to finish, she pulled out a whole handful of red licorice and chewed on one while her friend jabbered, every once in a while glancing at me, not knowing my tongue ached to taste just one mouthful of her licorice. Every time she looked at me, I wanted to evaporate. I had on a borrowed swimsuit a size too big, dull and old-fashioned compared to the bright-colored flower or print-covered two-pieces all the other girls wore. My hair hung down my back, straight and thick and dark.

The first girl said, "Look, this Indian is staring at us," and glared at me with icy blue eyes, her nose pointing to the ceiling. The second girl said, "Oh, she don't know what we're saying anyhow. Dirty Indians don't know anything." Her friend said, "I don't think she's really a real Indian. My dad says some of them are half-breeds. So she's not *all* dirty."

"Only half-dirty," her friend said, and they giggled together and laughed at me.

My face felt hot and my arms were heavy as I walked carefully across the wet, slippery floor towards them. I noticed from far away that the room's noises started to fade.

I grabbed one of them by her hair and threw her away, wrapped my arm around the other one's neck and wrestled her down, and sitting on her, I kept punching her till her friend grabbed me. I stood up, and jerking away, I tripped her, landing her by her friend. They were both still crying and screaming on the floor when I walked out, carrying my bundle of clothes under my arm.

Standing outside in the shade of the pool building, I was really scared. There was someone yelling, "Debi! Debi!" but I wouldn't look. Somehow I thought they found out my name and were going to do something to me. But it was my friend's mom; she and my friend went for popsicles and just got back. I ran to their car and told them what I did, so my friend's mom went in after the clothes my friend left in the shower room and we headed back for home.

Safe once again with my family, I told Mom and Dad I got in a fight.

"Daddy, what's a half-breed?" I asked him.

The house got quiet, the only sound was the wind. Daddy looked at me and his eyes were sad.

"My girl, you're an Indian. The way of living is Indian. Lakota."

I said, "Yes, but what is a half-breed?"

"A white man's word," is what he said. "It's just a white man's word."

Now, eighteen years later, I was wiping blood from my son's face, and his question made my body shake with anger, sadness, frustration and hatred. Opening my eyes, I answered, "You're Lakota, son. The way of living is Indian. You're Lakota."

44

He looked at me with black eyes shining with tears he now refused to shed, and asked me again what a half-breed was.

"A white man's word," is what I said. "It's just a white man's word."

Gretchen Cotrell

Letter to the Little Shell

This insatiable drive toward understanding has. . .created a consciousness in order to know what is and what happens, and in
order to piece together mythic conceptions from the slender hints
of the unknowable.

—C. G. Jung,
Memories, Dreams, Reflections

. . . a man (*sic*) who sees a different world with each eye is
paralyzed.

—Earl Shorris,
The Death of the Great Spirit

I.
You'd think I was crazy even if you didn't say it
If I told you I listen to war dances all day
& sit in a vision of Red Cloud, Crazy Horse, & Man Afraid
The swamps of sentimentality suck at my shoes
The prairies of October & all that
I was told not to talk about being part-Indian
& a lot of other things

II.
These days I wake up heavy
Coffee out of your cup tastes like wax
On the way back to my place I think of
The oncoming procession of guilty scenarios
I enter myself in the room I have created
Guiltily chopping the insanity from my life
I have made a room for my Indian blanket
Searching the ice floe for tongues
Looking for what happened

III.
I waited 'til I was 17 for a smartass farmboy to call me squaw
It had never quite occurred to me
This unprecedented taste of swamp water
I had to look suddenly down
& off to the left into the erotic confabulation
that separates politics from mythology

IV.
Who was she, your Saskatchewan Indian Grandmother
Who played & sang the mandolin like a bird
Thirty-some odd years dead, Grandmother
& one son tosses you off as a squaw
& the other one keeps saying you're white
I keep asking about you
& they keep saying they can't remember
Or it isn't polite to talk about it
They think you're part-Chippewa or Cree or both
Sometimes they say you're French-Canadian
Or even French 'n Indian
But most of the time they say it's just water under the bridge

What is the sign on the foreheads of Indians
In Montana   In the fifties
Of fullbloods Mixed bloods   Less than
Halfbreeds   Métis   Canadian Cree   Renegade Cree
White Indians passing
Redheaded redskinned frecklefaced Indians
Little white girls who grow up to be called squaw
What kind of slow wail for the empty valleys
Before the whites came

V.
The wolves howling again
Remind you of lies you know
You're a drifter
You have a short attention span
Homesick your life
Piled up around you like the fat of unread books
This silence does not belong to you
These corners in the street where the drunks hide
Without a lamp or a chair hoping no one will notice
You're thirty-three
You're still searching for the names of your Grandmothers

VI.
On the slow rise from L. A. to the High Mojave
I bear myself into the dreadful sweetness of the beginning
My life half over   After many times   For the first time
I'm going home to my people on the Eastern Side
Whom I have never seen
We are the survivors
There are no messages from California
We're supposed to be dead
Water under the   It is not
There are no messages

VII.
Each day moves me further north into misgivings & longing
To share this once in a lifetime

Lonely as lonely at Gull Point in the prehistoric mist
The sound of their crossing brings a moose & her calf
Washing over me the singing voices of Subarctic women

It is all right to go on

Drawing by Kawennotakie (Salli Benedict)

Alice Sadongei

What Frank, Martha and I Know About the Desert

My mother
used to speak about Coyote.
She talked to Praying Mantis—
asked him
when rain was coming.
She taught me, Frank and Martha
to look for sap
on the greasy bark
of mesquite.
(the sap has crunchy, crystalled edges, a smooth, wax-like center)
She told us
how to eat mesquite beans.
"gnaw on the ends, don't eat the seeds"
(the fiber inside the pod is sweet)
On zoo visits
we'd hear tales of Coyote.
"Coyote fell on desert sand
blinded by his vanity. Bluebird
laughed at him—now his coat is streaked and blotched."
Coyote knew
we were talking about him.
He'd let us look into his eyes.
My mother
would take me, Frank and Martha
to the desert in spring.
"Stand
alone out here.
Don't speak.
Listen
to the desert."

My mother
showed us a purple desert flower
that looked like a rabbit.
(they grow near the highway)
There are patches of poppies
near my grandfather's village.
Out there
in the desert
where there is nothing
but heat and the wobbly
shade of the mesquite
tree, look around before
you sit on a rock. There
may be lizards or snakes
sleeping under the cool
stone.

Charlotte DeClue

To the Spirit of Monahsetah

To the spirit of Monahsetah
and to all women who have
been forced to the ground.

(from the banks of the Konce)

there is death in this river
you can hear it speak.

the people fishing
or watching the great birds
nest in shallow coves
cannot hear it.
they have not been made to listen.

i have seen the eagles
and cast for fish

but there is something else here.
the Mystery that speaks
of life and death
and rebirth
has been stretched to its limits.
violence has imposed
new conditions

if i could
i would pull the death from this river.
if i could
i would fling it to the sky
but today the clouds hang
bruised and battered
as if saying
they too have had enough.

for downstream
a woman's body was found

delivered naked and nameless
into the river's lap.

my fingers claw wet clay
        touch earth   touch earth.
if you get lost
        touch earth.
if the wind changes directions
or you are caught midstream
        touch earth.

when violence hits you
        touch deep
for that is where it strikes.
the place
the moment
when the killer and his instrument
become one.

cold lifeless metal
held to my throat.
hand digging into pain.

i close my eyes to push
back the memory
but there is no stopping it.
no force of mind
no threat of retaliation.
(victims are stripped of will)

only the sheer nothingness
of a star breaking
into a million pieces
falling scattering.
and the sound
that only those who have heard
a star fall
can hear.

if i could
i would heal you Ushuaka
Woman's-self.
and we would walk again
without fear
without stumbling.

we would walk together
you and i
and talk about this and that.
(but not about what we have in common)

we could forget
and the river would be as it once was.

> at night
> the river flows silently
> past my bed
> while the full moon
> echoes across my floor
> > be whole again
> > little one.
> > be whole.

Wendy Rose

The Indian Women Are Listening: To the Nuke Devils

Your death, she said, is covered
like a bride might be covered
at a distance from her husband.
That is what the whiteman brought—
brides covered, things to hide,
and burning stones where each of us
must burn in blue Nevada canyons
words we cannot read.

I am your mother
and I tremble

> up from my blankets, shake and howl
> at you with hands outstretched in front
> to shield you or to push you ahead.

I come to take you
to the only place safe,
the only path going
to old age;

> pulling at the stakes I am angry still
> at the cross and nails, the hair they harvest
> from my hungry head. And if you push me

I will deny that
you are my daughter, you
who burst into this world
with the song of my belly,
my sisters' hands pulling;

you who beat your arms about you
chasing the heat futilely away.
This is my cry, my vision,
that you do not see me though
like fog I rise on all sides
about you, like rain
I feed your corn.
I am hungry enough
to eat myself and you,
for my blood runs from the river mouth,
from my bony banks flashfloods
bubble. I breathe on you again
to freeze you in one place, to catch you up
as you melt like grease and as I
tumble and whirl with arrows in my side,
antelope eyes open and wind blowing high
in fir and tamarack,
I topple the machinery
that rolls in the buffalo mounds,
break from electric trees
their tops, fall completely and forever
into star dust.

Lynn Randall

Grandma's Story

She never told me the year nor the season it happened. I don't even know what it's called in the history books, or if it's even in the history books. All I know is what she told me, and that Grandma called it "The Bombing Range Days."

She lay in bed that day, a little longer than usual. With nine kids underfoot and one on the way, the peace and quiet of the early morning hours were a luxury she seldom enjoyed. She thought about all the chores that needed to be done that day and the chores that were left over from yesterday. Mentally, she made a list assigning each child to a job. Still there were chores left to do. Chores that would probably be left over for tomorrow. Inwardly she groaned, rolling over and smothering any sound escaping into her pillow. Sighing wearily she got up to make coffee. Stepping carefully over the bodies of her children sprawled all over the floor, she made her way into the kitchen. She put the last of the wood into the stove. As she poured the kerosene and lit the stove, she decided to let her husband sleep a while before asking him to fetch more wood for the afternoon meal. She put the coffee on the stove and started to mix the batter for pancakes.

The sun was barely warming the earth when the man came. Her husband had risen an hour ago and was out back chopping wood. The sound of the knocking frightened her, none of her friends or neighbors ever knocked. They always yelled by the gate, and she ran out to meet them. The knocking continued. Backing away from the door, she bumped against her eldest son. "Take it easy Mom, I'll get it," he assured her. The man at the door stood tall. He was dressed in a green hat. This was the dress of an Army man. She knew this and it frightened her more. "Where's your man?" he demanded of her. She could only nod towards the back. The man turned to leave and she followed. She listened in silent rage as the man told her husband they had until nightfall to get their belongings together and get out. "It isn't fair," she thought. "First they take all the good land away from us and put us on this worthless tract of nothing-land; now they're taking that too." She listened on in new-found horror as the man explained what use the land would be to the Army. "New recruits need to be trained to fly and to know how to drop bombs. This worthless land will be perfect for this area of training. Tomorrow at eight o'clock, a squad of new recruits will be in for the first day of training." With that the man turned and left. She stared at her husband in shock and fear. Her husband's face reflected her own emotions. Together they quickly turned and ran toward the house, gathering objects as they ran.

Breathlessly she ran into the house shouting orders. Her oldest son, understanding immediately, ran out to help his father herd the cows together, heading them towards the boundary line. There wasn't much time and some would probably be lost or stolen before the day ended, but still they represented the food and money they would need later. The three oldest daughters started packing the household and personal items. The younger children were outside chasing and catching the hens and the old rooster, putting them in cardboard boxes, flour sacks, or whatever else would hold them. She ran out to hitch the team to the wagon. Almost immediately it began to fill. She started tearing apart the outhouse, throwing the planks down as she took them off. The wood was important, more useful than clothing, almost. Not paying attention to where she was walking, she stepped on a protruding nail. The nail was old and rusty. The pain was so great she found she couldn't stand on the foot for more than a few minutes. Sitting down, she cried in frustration, screaming at her children when they dared come close. Her husband, upon returning, found his wife sitting in the middle of a toilet, half-up half-down, crying her eyes out. He examined the wound then bandaged it with an old sheet he found, soothing her as he worked. Lifting her gently, he put her in the already filled wagon.

Together they raced across the country to the boundary line. As they neared the line, she stared in shock at what she saw. Her friends and neighbors were all over, unloading their wagons in a pile next to the fence, then jumping back into their wagons and racing off for the next load. Unlike the friendly faces she was used to, their faces were grim and determined. Her husband finished unloading, then took her off the wagon, setting her down next to the load. He raced off in the direction of the house. She looked at the sun, it was sitting dangerously close to the west. She only hoped they had time to get everything of importance. Looking around she saw her neighbors' belongings all along the fence. The older women were clearing out spaces for the tents. Some of the children were gathering wood for the fires. Suddenly she realized her family hadn't eaten since last night and started searching through her stuff for pots and pans and food. Sending her young son off for some wood, she began preparing the evening meal.

It was well into the night when her husband returned with the last load. The coffee was hot, the soup long since done. She just finished setting up the tent. Wearily she sat down, her leg throbbing in pain. Her swollen body ached with exhaustion. She watched as each of her children ate, then one by one crawled into the tent and to bed, till there was only herself and her husband. He hadn't said a word but only sat and stared into his coffee. Tears of frustration threatened her as she sat and looked at her husband. "What will happen now?" she asked. "Are we going to live on this hill, in this tent, the rest of our lives? Will we ever get to go back to our home?" He didn't answer her but only sat and stared into his cup. She looked at him for a while then put her head down and cried.

For as long as I can remember I heard my grandma tell this story. Sometimes a friend would drop over and together they would tell tales of that day with horror or amusement, whatever mood they were in. I can never tell the story as she told it. Each time she told it, she would be able to raise some emotion in me. I would laugh with her or I would cry with her. She left us last summer.

Terri Meyette

Celebration 1982

They say no one died.
Tiny desert flower
micro beetle bug
are they not life?
Their bag of bones
blown into the wind
captured in white dust storms
washed down polluted rivers
are they not dead?

They say no one died.
Scientist, unconscious
mushroom button pushers,
Secretary of Defense what's his name,
President what's his name
when will they be tried
for imposing fantasies and celebrations
on all life forms?

It wasn't enough
in "45"
Hiroshima and Nagasaki.

They say no one died.
Nevada desert
1000 miles into her bowels
earth melted.

radiation, radiation, radiation,
radiation.

oozed into blood
of Shoshone and Paiute.
The bomb lasted minutes
the intent lasts generations
in the womb of Creation, herself.

They say no one died.
Closing their eye,
they dismissed death
dismissed life
became blinded
by white flash
their God.

They say no one died.
As thousands of beetles
fell through the sky
and rabbit hair turned into
fur coats protecting atoms
as they floated into water.
They won't look
they will just say
no one died.

Winona LaDuke

"They always come back"

An *Interview with Winona LaDuke. Previously published in* Science for the People, *897 Main Street, Cambridge, MA 02139.*

SP: *In what ways does uranium mining affect native peoples?*

LaDuke: Let's start with an example. In 1952, the Anaconda Co. discovered uranium at the village of Paguate on the Laguna Pueblo Reservation. Two decades later, Anaconda held claim to the largest uranium strip-mine operation in the world. The Jackpile Mine provided the people of Laguna Pueblo with a healthy tribal treasury and much-needed employment. Then in 1981, when the mining cycle inevitably turned from boom to bust, the Anaconda Co. decided its job, along with the jobs of the Laguna, was finished. With the closure of the Jackpile Mine, the Laguna people face some stark problems, which, unlike their benefactor, the Anaconda Co., won't disappear.

In 1973, the EPA came to visit the Laguna Pueblo and found that the Rio Paguate River was contaminated with radiation from the Jackpile Mine, as was most of the groundwater near the village of Paguate. During a second visit, in 1975, the EPA found that not only in Laguna Pueblo, but throughout the entire mining region of the Southwest, the groundwater was heavily contaminated with radiation.

In 1978, when EPA officials returned for the last time, they determined that several of the buildings at the Pueblo were contaminated with radiation. The community center, the Jackpile Housing Project, and the tribal council headquarters had all been constructed with radioactive materials from the mine.

Because of the groundwater contamination, the drinking fountain at a rest stop on highway I-40 has been fitted with a special water purifier, which removes particles of radionuclides. Visitors, people passing through, don't have to worry, but the nontransient populations of Acoma, Laguna, and Dine Indians aren't so lucky.

SP: *How does the water become contaminated? By a slow process of rain leaching radioactive materials from tailing dumps?*

LaDuke: That's part of the problem, but there have been major accidents at the uranium milling plants. The United Nuclear Company's Churchrock accident, which followed Three Mile Island by four months, occurred when an impoundment dam busted open. One hundred million gallons of highly radioactive water and 1,100 tons of mill tailings were immediately released into the Rio Puerco River, near Grants, New Mexico. The company had known that the dam was faulty; it had cracked two years prior to the break.

The Dine community of Churchrock was immediately affected by the spill!. Animals became so contaminated with radiation that their internal organs completely deteriorated. Since the Dine depended on the animals, particularly the sheep, for their subsistence, their supply of food as well as water was eliminated. Young children were brought to Los Alamos for radiation counts, but the studies were conducted inappropriately and inadequately.

Despite the fact that it was the worst spill of radioactive materials in U.S. history, the Churchrock accident received minimal press coverage. Perhaps the press and Kerr-McGee thought that because the accident occurred in an area of low population, where radiation levels were already quite high, it was not really news. If the same spill had happened in a wealthy white community, the media might have responded differently.

SP: *Presumably, Grants isn't the only area where Native Americans have to drink contaminated water.*

LaDuke: No, not at all. On the Pine Ridge Sioux Reservation in South Dakota, there's serious contamination. Federal maximum acceptable radiation dosages are two picocuries per liter of water. Several areas of Pine Ridge average between 19 and 25 picocuries per liter.

In December of 1979, 38 percent of all pregnancies on Pine Ridge resulted in miscarriages before the fifth month, or excessive hemorrhaging, and 60-70 percent of the children who were born suffered breathing problems caused by under-developed lungs and jaundice. Francis Wise, a young Indian lawyer who works with women on the reservation, decided they had to do something about it.

The women of Pine Ridge began door-to-door surveys and scientific investigations of their environment. In March of 1980, Women of all Red Nations (WARN), an organization based in the area, released a preliminary study. The WARN study indicated that the reservation water contained pollutants from virtually every imaginable source. A major source was the two-hundred-gallon spillage of uranium wastes from an abandoned mill in the nearby town of Edgemont, combined with the runoff from carcinogenic defoliants used in the area. To complicate matters, Ellsworth Air Force Base, which uses one-eighth of the reservation as a bombing range, was contributing its share of pollutants, all of which were flowing into the water the people drink.

Subsequent investigations and a series of Freedom of Information Act requests verified what WARN feared. Indian Health Service records obtained through the FOIA revealed that between 1971 and 1979, 314 babies had been born with birth defects in a total population of 12,500 Indians.

SP: *Could you give us an idea of the scope of the problem nation-wide or globally?*

LaDuke: The major uranium deposits under production in the world today are in North America, and the U.S. and Canada are the two leading producers; most of the deposits are in Saskatchewan, Ontario, New Mexico, and Wyoming. Other major producers are South Africa and Namibia, followed by Australia.

Without exception, uranium is located on the remaining land base of the indigenous people of these areas; and, without exception, these people, either as uranium miners or as the settled population, are getting the hell radiated out of them.

Two-thirds of all North American uranium is located on or adjacent to Indian reservations. In aboriginal Australia, the figures are the same. Millions of acres of Canadian reserves are under lease for mining exploration.

Radiation poisoning is fast becoming the main food of native peoples. And . . . in the name of economic and military security . . . control, occupation, and guns are the butter on the bread of oppression required to maintain uranium production. In Namibia, for example, South Africa maintains 70,000 government troops. In North America police forces in the form of FBI or Bureau of Indian Affairs SWAT teams are periodically brought in to protect uranium deposits and reinforce security at the mines.

SP: *Would you say that uranium mining is a major cause of the oppression of native peoples?*

LaDuke: Uranium itself is not what downpresses people. The downpression of native people is linked to the subjugation and exploitation of the Earth. With each generation, the techno-industrial system creates demands for more resources from the land. First it was land for agricultural crops, then for gold, then for iron, then for oil, and now uranium.

Because native people, or land-based, nonurban populations, are closest to the Earth, our fate is directly related to the fate of the Earth . . . much more so than for an urban population which has buffered itself by means of a need-production-supply chain and a set of technological accouterments to meet immediate physical demands.

An event like a black-out, which both causes and adversely affects the technological basis of urban, industrial society, may be regarded as an environmental crisis in urban and suburban America: for a moment, technology seems an enemy to consumers of techno-culture, but soon the lights are back on. For a native land-based population, in contrast, an environmental crisis is the flooding of one hundred thousand square miles of northern Quebec Indian reserves for a hydroelectric project that keeps the lights bright in New York City. There's a big difference.

There is a clear historical pattern to the subjugation of native people, which, like the subjugation of the natural environment, is at least four hundred years old in this hemisphere. It is even older in Europe. What the church and state have done in the Western Hemisphere has clear historical origins in the behavior of the same institutions in Europe. In both hemispheres, the exploitation of native peoples has expanded geometrically, not linearly. The subjugation, exploitation, and genocide of native peoples is structural, or systemic, in the development of the world.

To native peoples, there is no such thing as the first, second, and third worlds; there is only an exploiting world . . . whether its technological system is capitalist or communist . . . and a host world. Native peoples, who occupy more land, make up the host world.

Water, land, and life are basic to the natural order. All else has been created by the use and misuse of technology. It is only natural that in our respective struggles for survival, the native peoples are waging a war to protect the land, the water, and life, while the consumer culture strives to protect its technological lifeblood.

This protective pattern of response can be seen in Euro-American communities confronting the current crisis in the disposal of toxic and hazardous waste. For the most part, they focus on containing, regulating, or controlling this insidious pollution, rather than on eliminating the problem at its source.

The aboriginal peoples of Australia illustrate the conflict between technology and the natural world succinctly, by asking, "What will you do when the clever men destroy your water?" That, in truth, is what the world is coming to.

SP: *What about the coverage of Native issues in the press?*

LaDuke: It's terrible. The desecration of the planet and of native peoples is hidden away in the back pages of the newspapers. Because the natural environment is not economically influential, politically prestigious, or fashionable, what happens to it cannot percolate into the information bank of the general population. The same can be said of the people who live closest to the natural environment . . . native people. Native people have not attracted enough popular interest to be accorded a piece of the popular mind.

For instance, the brutal struggle for a free trade union movement in Bolivia receives no press coverage by the U.S. Media, Inc., liberal or not, while Poland is in the world's eye. And on the subject of the MX missile system . . . while nuclear-arms proliferation and the gross financial obesity of the Defense Dept. receive massive amounts of media attention, the residents of Nevada . . . the Shoshone Indians . . . and their struggle against the MX remain invisible. And if white America has long been guilt-ridden because of a recurring "Indian problem," white America is also guilt-ridden because of a recurring environmental problem. The white American system . . . and finally, white America itself . . . relate to both of these problems in the same way: by ignoring them. As far as the crises of water contamination, radiation, and death to the natural world and its children are concerned, "respectable racism" is as alive today as it was a century ago.

SP: *Could you say more about this racism?*

LaDuke: Simply, a certain level of racism and ignorance has gained acceptance . . . in fact, respectability. Like the wealthy who think of Blacks only as house servants and believe they are doing these people a favor by providing them with a clean job in a good family, the consumers of technoculture relate to the native and the environment in terms of master, servant, house. We either pick your bananas or act as mascot for your football team. In this way, respectable, enlightened people are racist. They are arrogant toward all of nature, arrogant toward the children of nature, and ultimately arrogant toward all of life.

The point is that Euro-Americans perceive the development of their culture as a mastery of the natural world, a prime example of the progress from primitive to civilized society. They seem to believe that this culture is either immune to ecological disasters, or clever enough to survive them. This is racism, founded on the precarious conception of the technological and mental superiority of the consumer-producer system.

Racism, oppression, and death are integral components of the resource development process, and they are all contained within the mining, milling, and technological use of uranium. That's why natural people watch with dismay as concern about uranium mining in the general population steadily diminishes, and the issue of nuclear power fizzles out as the issue of nuclear weaponry grows. As Don Morton, a white political exile from South Africa, has said, "If we could win the struggle to keep uranium in the ground, then we would have indeed sliced the head off the nuclear industry and weapons threat."

SP: *Do you think it's possible to win that struggle?*

LaDuke: Well, if we are to listen to U.S. economists, either progressive or conservative, the uranium mining industry is going bust. All of the big plans for mining expansion look like the delirious hallucinations of gluttons who ate too much. A 1979 joint report by the OECD Nuclear Energy Agency and the International Atomic Energy Agency predicted that the 368 operating mines in the U.S. would double their 1979 production levels by 1985, that Canadian production would also double; that South African production would be maintained; and that Australian production would increase twenty times by the end of the decade.

But in the last three years, the exchange value of uranium has dropped rapidly, from $43.25 per pound in late 1978 to $23 recently. The crash in the price of uranium has precipitated a halt to innumerable mining ventures around the globe and forced a number of mines across the U.S. to close. Needless to say, all the experts in the nuclear industry look a little bit stupid.

Unfortunately, one would have to be even more delirious than the gluttonous uranium/nuclear industry to believe that, if the mines close down, the problem will simply disappear.

The symptoms of the problem . . . nuclear power and weapons . . . won't disappear either. If the industry doesn't have enough uranium now to make the planet totally uninhabitable, it can always use those precious strategic stockpiles of ore, or reopen the mines and start all over again.

So when the people who live in the Grants mineral belt and elsewhere in uranium country see the mines close down, they say, "They'll come back again. They always come back for more." They remember that before the uranium, it was coal; before that, it was oil, gold, copper, and silver.

There is a critical difference between the native's mentality and the visitor's mentality; that is, the mentality of the industry. The visitor moves from resource to resource, from mine to mine, from factory to factory, assaulting the Earth and the Earth's people, and leaving behind skeletons. The native, nontransient population has no option to move or evacuate.

The native has no choice but to act in defense of the native community and the natural environment. And episode after episode of native people's resistance to technoculture permeates the nuclear era. On May 29, 1980, a group of Ketchi Indians went to the mayor at Panzos, Guatemala, insisting that their land be returned to them. The Guatemalan army was waiting, and opened fire: three hundred natives were massacred. The incident was much like the massacre of three hundred Indians at Wounded Knee a century before. It is the same war.

In the Black Hills of South Dakota, a group of Lakota have liberated an area of their sacred lands from government ownership. In April 1980, the Lakota began to resettle in the hills, in an effort to establish a self-sufficient community. Yellow Thunder Camp has met with military surveillance, terrorism, and harassment. The governor of South Dakota, William Janklow, has accelerated an aggressive anti-Indian campaign, but the group remains undaunted.

The land war in North America continues, but, perhaps because it is so close, so real, and so disguised by the collective racism, downpression, and callousness of the American consumer, it is not noticed by most.

The native sees that the system may drift and change, but it must always come back to the land for its food. That means it must come back to land-based peoples. For that reason, the system and the native have always been, and will always be, enemies.

Janice Gould

Dispossessed

I remember in October
driving to the mountains,
the kids piled in the back of the pick-up,
tucked under sleeping bags and blankets.
We drank coffee from a thermos
spiked with a slug of brandy.
There was already snow
on the north face of the ridges,
a storm chased flocks of migrant birds south.
We were headed for Maidu country.
Maples had yellow leaves,
a clear, cold breeze
blew through the canyon,
there was frost on the meadows in the morning,
woodsmoke and mist in the evening.
At the new tavern
built on the homestead
where my mom once lived,
two Indian girls drank beer
and played pool with some white guys.
They looked at me strangely
when we came in,
and what should seem familiar
was foreign and strained.
This is not my land anymore.
The creek where Mama played,
the graveyard up the hill
that lies beneath the hum
of massive power lines,
the cabin with its spirit children—
these things are not mine.

Geraldine Keams

Canyon Day Woman Blues

Woman III (Jessie)

The coffee,
The cigarettes,
All day long.
She reads the papers.
Never finds interesting news.

Bored,
She watches headlines,
Slowly burn in the fireplace.
Watches T.V. every night
Because there's nothing else to do.
Sometimes,
Staring into darkness . . .
Nothingness . . .
Waiting for the dawn.

Woman IV (Leona)

Goes to work at eight.
Wears the same dress every day.
The gingham, in hues of lavender and grey.
She's built like a box.
Weighing at least two hundred, maybe more.
She likes to go to Kung-Fu movies.
And has hangovers just about every weekend.

Elizabeth Cook-Lynn

A Family Matter

A vague restlessness woke Anita, and on impulse she got up and opened the bedroom window. It was just before dawn when the light of the moon had faded and shadows fell darkly upon the steep hills and pines and the river lay silent and still. Today she was going to Fort Hall.

Crouching on her knees, Anita peered into the darkness and felt the presence of the geese just before she heard them. Hurrying, stroking the air powerfully, purposefully, the huge flock hung for a moment above her window and then, individually, they began their lonely awkward cries to each other, calling their names and telling their stories and moving ponderously into the heavy fog which lay in the distance across the hills. Unaccountably, hot tears stung Anita's eyes and her nose. Her cheeks ached. Quickly, she got up and switched on a light in the hall and went to the kitchen to make coffee.

She poured the hot coffee into a thermos and went back to the bedroom and dressed in the semi-darkness. She went over to her husband, motionless in the pretense of sleep, his arms raised to cover his eyes. "I'm going," she said. She sat still on the side of the bed for a few moments, until she realized that he wasn't going to say anything to her and then she put on her coat, took the thermos from the kitchen table and left the house. She drove her car carefully away in the drizzling rain and she knew that Ray was lying there listening to her leave.

An hour later she stopped just outside of St. Maries and parked her red Nova at a rest stop alongside the freeway. It's the first of November, she thought, and she felt chilled as she walked to the roadway bathroom, the sky and the land shrouded in gray light. She searched the sky for the sun, weak and pale beneath the moist clouds, and decided silently, this day's not going to get any better than this.

The toilet was empty except for a short, white-haired woman who smiled and adjusted her belt as Anita walked to the narrow booth. "Too much coffee, I guess," said the white-haired lady pleasantly and they both nodded.

Moments later as they left the bleak quiet bathroom the woman smiling brightly said do you mind if I ask you a question sure said Anita you're Indian aren't you yes well said the woman I've known a lot of good Indians and there's nothin' to be ashamed of we're from Phoenix as if that explained something and we run a grocery and tourist stop and we've had a lot of good Indian boys work for us you don't need to be ashamed of that.

In order not to be rude, Anita strolled with the woman to the curb and feigned a politeness she did not feel.

70

"Where you headed?" asked White Hair.

"Fort Hall."

"Oh, do you live there?"

"No. I used to be married there. I'm just going there to get my two sons and bring them back with me."

"Oh, how nice! Well," said White Hair, who noticed that her husband had started the car engine, "have a nice trip," and she smiled and waved.

Anita felt small and remote as she pulled onto the freeway, and the whistling wind rising about the faulty car window reminded her of the sound of huge goose wings flapping. White Hair's "how nice" hissed in her ears and she tried to organize her vision about herself as the mother of her two sons and the wife of Ray and the ex-wife of Victor and the daughter-in-law of Rosina and the stepdaughter of John Thunder and . . . and . . . she tried to organize these thoughts about herself around White Hair's recognition though she knew it to be superficial and secular. How nice that I'm going to get my sons . . . after a year's rehab at the treatment center and two years working as a nurse's aide and two years married to Ray. How nice! For five years my sons haven't laid eyes on me and now I'm going to get them. How nice!!

"Rain is expected to continue," the radio announcer proclaimed. "Highs will be around fifty to fifty-four degrees throughout the day and lows are expected to reach twenty-eight degrees. And now, here's George Jones, the best of the country singers and he's fallen on hard times, with 'He Stopped Loving Her Today.'"

Anita thought vaguely about her own decline and weary deterioration and considered that it had been as inevitable, perhaps, as the fading of the dim November sun she now glimpsed over her left shoulder as she drove, the yellow outlines of the great tunkashina impotent and moving away from the Earth, feeble and indistinct.

As the rain glittered and country music filled the air, the red Nova slipped through the hills of Northern Idaho and the hours passed and the woman driving did not stop but once for gas until the headlights fell upon one of the three grocery stores at Fort Hall, Idaho. She bought some cheese, crackers, and milk and went straight to the motel to eat a quick snack and fall into a heavy, soundless sleep.

Toward morning she dreamed of two small boys walking along looking for a bear. While they were walking they heard something coming after them. When they looked around they saw that it was their mother's head. "Where are you going?" asked the head. The children became afraid and ran away and climbed into a tree. Their mother's head followed them and began shaking the tree and just when the tree was about to fall, a voice from the treetop said to the children, "Sit, quickly, in the bird nest," and as they climbed into the bird's nest, the wind bore it off swiftly. The head wept loudly.

Anita woke with a start as the weeping sounds of her dream changed to the murmur of autumn wind moaning in her ears and she lay in the narrow bed, exhausted and spent. She thought about Ray and wished that he would have consented to come with her.

Leaves swept in bunches covered the sidewalk as she entered the tribal building and asked the secretary to confirm her appointment with Emil White Horn and the tribal family counselors.

When she walked into the court chambers she noticed that her children were not present, only their grandmother, Rosina, and she felt sharply disappointed for a moment. Then she felt her hands go cold as she realized that something was wrong.

She looked up and scanned the judge's chambers and she saw Emil striding toward her and as he held out his hand to her, he said, "Anita, something's happened here. You see, the boys didn't want to come and they don't want to see you and so we've got them in Smokey's office down the hall. We thought we'd just go ahead and hear some testimony and maybe . . . you know . . . these family matters . . ."

"No," cried Anita and she jerked her hand away from him. "They're MY KIDS and nobody's going to turn them against me and it's already been decided that they would come with me . . ."

"Look, Anita," pleaded Emil. "Jesus Christ, it's been, how long? Five, six years? Jesus, Anita, give those kids a chance. They don't even know you."

"That's not it, Emil, that's not it." Panic rose in her. "You know that's not it. That old woman, there . . ." and she pointed to the children's grandmother, Victor's mother, Rosina, "She's the one! She's turned them against me. She never did like me and she has made them afraid of me. That's what's happened."

By this time, Anita was moving down the hall toward the office where her children were being held. Rosina, silent and fearful, moved along with her, the two women now facing each other, Emil being drawn behind them as though sleepwalking. Finally, Emil found his voice and said, "Anita, come into the judge's chambers here and we can talk about this . . ."

Now Anita had reached Smokey's office and, turning her attention inward, she softly opened the door and saw her two sons, almost grown, Jay Richard, he was three when she last held him in her arms and Victor, Jr., she had always called him Chunskay, had been four when she had last seen him. Looking at them as though from a great distance she knew what fine men they would become and tears welled in her throat. She drew in her breath and with great restraint she said their names softly. As she stood before them she could see the fear and hatred in their eyes and she said, "Don't be afraid," and then, "You know me, don't you?"

Young Victor pulled Jay Richard to him as his mother reached out toward them and they both pressed themselves against the corner of the desk.

"Oh, My God," said Anita. "Look what she's done. Look what she's done to them." And she moved her hands toward her forehead and wiped the perspiration away. She stroked the hair at her temples in a gesture of anguish. Still looking at her sons, she began speaking in the tribal language of her ancestors:

"taku iniciapi he? ni Dakotapi!
You are my sons and you are Dakotahs
and your relatives are significant
people. You must remember who you
are!"

It was a plea, but Jay Richard and Victor Jr. looked back at her uncomprehendingly. Slowly they moved toward their grandmother and each took a position beside her and, finally, Chunskay said to the mother he had forgotten, "We do not want to go with you. Don't make us go with you."

The misery in the young mother's eyes was too much for Emil, himself moved almost to tears, and he took her arm and led her into the hallway.

His voice choked with emotion, he said, "Look, Anita . . . we can work this out . . . we'll have to . . ."

But before he could finish, Anita lifted her head and pushed his arm away and said, "No . . . no . . ." and she walked away from him. She didn't look back at him as she left the building, though, if she had, she would have seen that his eyes were filled with sorrow.

As she drove north she noticed that the snow had started. Soft, large flakes streaked and slanted through the air like a funnel with its tip just in front of her eyes. A long column of geese zigzagged through the gray sky toward her, and just before it fell away, she thought it seemed close enough to touch.

Share Ouart

Letter from Prison

Jan 10, 1983

Dear Beth,

I received your letter and it was a very nice letter. It was nice to get a letter for a change.

I left home at an early age because I felt unwanted and a burden. My mother had 5 daughters. I felt the hate she felt for my father. I think my first husband was a replacement for a father for me. He was 11 years older. I just wanted love all the time. I worked as a waitress and had a room at a hotel and was on my own before I moved in with my first X. I rode horseback over 600 miles to where I decided to live on my own from my mother. I had been running away since I was 4 and had been jailed for it at 11. Everything in my past practically is depressing except my children.

You sound like your children are the main meaning of your life too?

I've been thinking of taking the kids to yellow thunder camp in the Black Hills of S. Dakota where I am from. When I get out. I want them to realize the value of nature and know there heritage and all that goes with it. Theres a gold mine in the Black Hills where I worked before. I hope to get on there. I have a good record there and it pays enough that I can make it ok. Its very hard work but I am strong and with my lack of education its best pay I will be able to get.

I found the system very unbearable when I first came in. I took a overdose of pills at the county jail and one week later gashed my inner elbow to the bone. Its so awful being away from my children plus all the humiliation. 75% of the staff here is Black. I am considered white by them. It is so strange. I am use to being last and ridiculed, but it is funny to be considered white.

This is hopefully the bottom. I am sure I will never get my older son back and everything is at an alltime worst. So hopefully its up from here. I know that never a day will pass that I don't give thanks for my freedom and my 2 children I have. I think I might enjoy independence. I've been married literly ½ my life. When I get out I will be like you, single.

I don't have my health. This long battle has took its toll. I hope I am not back here for stealing my son again. that would be rough on my other 2. I fear I'll be back in here with a murder charge like my sioux sister, Rita. I don't know why Oklahoma is so hard on sioux womens children. My mother always said whites would steal indian babies. I thought she meant because of my learning english, etc., now maybe I do know what she meant. I should of never left the Rosebud Res.

as long as I draw a breath,
Share

WOMAN WARRIOR.

© JAUNE QUICK-TO-SEE SMITH 1984

Alice Bowen

Circumstance

sweet, sweet wine
make me forget
the decay of heart
that raped the land
killed our intimate friends

sweet, red wine
cherished warmth
making existence bearable
on this once
beautiful land

cheap, sour wine
comfort
console me
I stand stripped
of dignity,
and wise, old ways

Canada's *Natural* Resource

despair inspires me, moods guide my hand
to trap the words upon a page
untangling thoughts
making them concrete

sometimes, no one gives a damn
sometimes, i see that middle-class dream
of some   (not me)   fade before my eyes
and know that i'm gonna die one day

maybe a bullet from the fbi

maybe at my own hands

cause this time the despair was too much.

"So tractable, so peaceable are these people," Columbus wrote, "that I swear to your majesties there is not in the world a better nation. They love their neighbors as themselves and their discourse is ever sweet and gentle, and accompanied by a smile; and though it is true that they are naked, their manners are decorous and praiseworthy. . . . [They must be] made to work, sow and do all that is necessary to adopt our ways."

This ironic twist of logic is not unusual, but rather commonplace in the history of Canadian relations with Native people. Although both the British and the French began with different approaches to the indigenous people, they both desired to rid themselves of what was termed the "Indian problem."

One of the first in a long line of experiments designed to change Native ways was the Sillery reserve, set up in Quebec in 1635. It was designed to segregate Indians so they would become sedentary farmers and adopt the ways of the white man. It was described by author Kathleen Jamieson as "a laboratory with a missionary-controlled environment, in which the desired changes could be effected."

Missionaries soon had total control of all religious and educational institutions for Native people.

Later, treaties were signed and reserves were designated for Indian occupancy. Francis Bond-Head, Lieutenant Governor of Upper Canada in 1836, saw reserves as a place of internment, until this endangered species faded from memory like the dodo. He felt that "Indians were a doomed race and melting like snow before the sun." "The greatest kindness," Bond-Head said, "that we can perform for these intelligent, simple-minded people, is to remove and fortify them as much as possible from all contact with the whites."

Despite his predictions, the Native population, which has increased by 40 percent during the last 20 years, is now the fastest growing of any minority in Canada.

LEGISLATIVE DISCRIMINATION

The Indian Act, passed in 1876, has jurisdiction over "Indians and the land reserved for the Indians." Although slightly amended, in essence it is still the same as 106 years ago.

The descendents of those who did not sign a treaty or become registered are not legally recognized as "Indians." This document has become legislated discrimination, and is used as a means to "divide and conquer" Native people. Those who have status are separated by law from those who don't.

Having signed treaties, the government changed its course of action. They encouraged enfranchisement, the forfeiting of one's legal status as an Indian, to accelerate assimilation. This allowed the government to relinquish their monetary commitments to treaty Indians. Until 1960, Indians could not vote or buy liquor and had to reside on the reserve to retain our treaty status. Conditioned to believe that our culture was worthless, Native people believed there was no value in being Indian.

Enfranchisement held the promise of acceptance and equality in Canadian society. This policy, combined with government and church oppression, contributed to the breakdown of Native culture and identity. This has resulted in a disintegrated society and loss of pride, self-respect, and motivation for the individual and community. "It's this sense of hopelessness," says Dr. Diane Syers of the Toronto East General Hospital's Crisis Unit, "that one finds so pervasive in the lives of so many Native people. They feel there is nothing to look forward to, no future. They feel overwhelmed by circumstances and often try to escape into an oblivion induced by alcohol." These feelings of powerlessness and rejection often result in the ultimate protest . . . suicide. Dr. Syers found that almost all cases of on-reserve suicide were alcohol-related and that "25 percent involved alcoholics." Combining alcohol with other problems, Syers says, "is analogous to a ticking bomb . . . a socially isolated, dependent person, with very low self-esteem, who is eventually swept away by emotions one cannot control."

PROFITABLE NATURAL RESOURCE

The Department of Indian Affairs magazine, *Indian Conditions*, states that the suicide rate among Native people is three times the national rate. Suicides also account for 35 percent of "accidental deaths" in the 15-24 age group, and 21 percent in the 25-34 age group. The study concludes that "approximately 50-60 percent of illness and death among Natives is alcohol-related."

Alcohol abuse is also responsible for the disproportionate amount of Native people in prisons. For the last two hundred years, Indians have had a history of alcohol-related offenses. Today, most crimes by Natives are still linked to alcohol, so much so it almost excludes other types of crime. From examining current statistics, four basic premises may be made:

1. An extremely large proportion (85 percent) of offenses involve alcohol, either directly or indirectly.
2. Crimes committed against the property are usually impulsive and clumsy in execution. The offender has usually been drinking.
3. Crimes committed against the person reflect covert hostility, which becomes overt with the use of alcohol.
4. There is little evidence of crime involving embezzlement, organized crime or involvement with drugs.

A 1979 inquiry by the Ontario Native Council on Justice revealed the minimum clear profit received by the government from the sales of alcohol to Natives was 25 million dollars. Only 4 percent, $5.50 per capita, was returned to Native alcohol treatment centers.

Angus Reid, of the University of Manitoba, conducted an intensive study of 367 Canadian alcohol treatment facilities in 1976. He found "that funding for Native people is substantially lower on a per capita basis than it is for whites . . . by about one-half."

Native alcoholics have become a profitable "natural resource," and are exploited as a business. They justify thousands of jobs in treatment facilities and correctional centers. Self-determination and independence for Native people would mean profit loss and unemployment for these "professionals."

Most alcohol counselors, both Indian and white, conduct programs based on European concepts of rehabilitation. This further contributes to the process of acculturation and the loss of our identity and independence.

Treatments rooted in European philosophies cannot restore self-sufficiency to Native people. It is the traditional medicine people and the elders who have the knowledge, who teach us what was lost to us through cultural genocide.

"Alcoholics think they've got control of the bottle, but it has taken them to places they don't want to go: hospitals, institutions and jails," says Vern Harper, president of Wandering Spirit Survival School, a Native-way school in Toronto. "Teaching our children Native values will prevent alcoholism. We have to start now, when they are young . . . instead of being left to pick up the pieces. Retaining our culture will turn the cycle of dependence around."

Mary Moran

I picked up your cast away hide

In the first season
you cloaked my primed rage.
I felt your claws
dig into my arms
marking the bloodline deeper.

My back slumps heavy
into this second winter.
You clothe me thick
with your closeness.

Your scalp pulls at my right temple,
reminder of the gaping hole in your skull.
A chip of bone flung aside.
The cougar springs out with a harsh,
high-pitched scream that no one hears.

I call for a shaman.
I reach for the medicine woman.
Your skin begins to graft
around my wrists and neck
as I build the daily fire
and wait.

---

written for my brother who died 10/17/80
with a bullet in his head.

Denise Panek

evelyn searching

(to my sister evelyn)

Could i tell you how it is
to search the vacant faces
like lockers at a bus station,

to spend three days and two nights
waiting for the right time
to say   father   or even   sister?

would it even matter if i said
the looking and the finding
could split you in two
send you into empty caverns
of silence   fearful of the
sound of your own voice?

I can stand long and far
from that punishing storm
and see in you how strangers
become fathers become strangers
in time and of choice
and how we return and we will
as daughters
as mothers lifting the children
above our heads
to change the color of the sky.

Kate Shanley

Returning

The jackfish in dry death
comes back in our dream,
his rasping breath
a rotting odor between us.
You remember, don't you?
He was a gift
from our neighbor
    "My son caught it today
    On the Red, down by the dike.
    You like fish, don't you?"
The old woman riddled by a hunger
seventy years of hunger
and ten children, one
retarded, one a drunk, two dead.
    "Me, I can't eat it no more . . .
    the bones they stick
    in my throat, but you
    young folks . . ."
So, I carried it home at arm's
length, the slope of the dishpan
too steep for its leaping.

Come and see—He's alive!
I told you.
We stood around him and stared.
Neither one of us could kill him,
his dark, cold eye echoing
our own dumb scream.
We shut the door on the porch
and waited in the dim light.
In the morning I wrapped it
in old newspapers,
and took it to the trash.
My son cried because
the jackfish was dead.

We did not speak, you and I,
for days—now he's back.
And at night we swim murky waters
with the knife. We know
next time we must feel
the bone cracking. We must
feel the blood gush wet
washing us back
into the stream.

Luci Tapahonso

The Trees Along the River

I'll wait until I've circled
the sloping curve of cliffs past Mesita—
the sun is so bright at the top
shining right in my eyes.
Squinting, I pull the visor down
and look off to the side
smooth, red cliffs   now
I'll light a cigarette.

At the Laguna Tribal Building,
I said   I want to see the governor
and 3 men said all at once
I'm the governor
and we all laughed.

The trees along the river
by the trading post have turned a fiery gold
against the gray banks covered
with dry brown weeds that are
dying for the winter.

Inside the warm kitchen, she was
mixing bread dough and she stopped
saying   You know, down at the
post office, there were some people
with a case of beer in their pickup
and someone told the police. The
police made them pour it all out—
they didn't even arrest them!
We just complained about that!
The tribal police don't do what
they should these days. Then she said
Have some piñons—there's lots
this year.

Coming back, the sun was setting
in my sideview mirror—a square of brilliant orange
hovering at the corner of my eye
wanting my attention over and over again.

Audrey LaForme

The Lamp in the Window

May stood at the top of the stairs. She watched the shadows of her Grandmother and Aunt Garnet cast by the lamp on the oil-spattered wall. Pulling her worn sweater around her, she stooped to sit on the top stair. It was late but she pushed back the tired longing creeping into her arms and legs. She didn't want to lie down, and she didn't want to think about last night. But she did.

Zea, her grandmother, and Aunt Garnet had left the house after dark to help husk the corn at the longhouse. Before closing the porch door they told her that if anyone came by she was to set the lamp back in the window and they would be right home. May snapped the wooden latch down to let her grandmother know she had locked the door, hesitated a few moments then leaned close to the door and listened. Satisfied that they were gone she eased a crack in the door. Opening it wider she could see the tiny glow of the cigarette Aunt Garnet had lit before the door closed. She listened and could hear the fading of their footsteps on the bare path. She knew the path would take them along its dips and curves, and up to the clearing where the longhouse stood. They lived that close.

May walked back into the kitchen and closed the door that separated the room from the porch. She leaned against the door for a few moments before deciding to check the fire in the woodstove. It was while she stoked the flames that she began to be afraid.

May had always been a little afraid of the dark. Sometimes she had to get up and go to the outhouse during the night. On the way back she could feel her body pushing itself towards the door. Often she wouldn't resist that terrible urging and she would run from the shadows, away from that unseen demon. In the morning she would feel foolish and ashamed. She never told anyone.

May pulled back the thick quilt on her Grandmother's cot, undressed and lay very still. The crackling of the wood had stopped; it would simmer until morning. There was no sound. May felt that she would be okay if she could only hear some sound. Flinging back the covers May jumped up and stood beside the woodstove. She reached for the worn poker that hung on a nail. Lifting the round, black lid she poked through the top layer of ash until the wood underneath cracked and snapped back to life. Still, she could feel herself becoming afraid, quite afraid. She realized she was afraid of dying.

A few weeks before, Zea had begun singing a soft, lifting tune as they washed their clothes on the porch. She taught May the Indian words first, then sang the song in English:

See them fly,
See them fly,
When I die,
I, too, will fly.

May learned the English words too and thought it sad that the song lost some of its meaning when she sang it in English. It sounded less pretty. It was at this time May realized her grandmother would die someday. And it was with fear and horror that May realized that she, too, would die. That night she had crept down the stairs long after Zea and Aunt Garnet were asleep. She sat in the rocking chair, in its deep, grey corner, and finally fell asleep before the morning.

And, last night, alone, May felt the same fear.

It came upon her like a thick, heavy blanket, pressing in from all sides, squeezing the breath from her. She let the lid fall back into place and threw the poker into the wood box. Whirling around she seized the lamp from its tiny stand and set it down in the window. She was breathing now, but it was long, drawn gasps. It was as if she had been working very hard. She stood back and watched the wick flicker within the globe. She looked past the reflection in the window pane and peered into the darkness, seeing nothing but feeling relieved. May went up the stairs and lay on her bed. She fell asleep waiting for her Grandmother and Aunt Garnet to get home.

She awoke to the sound of steps going back down the stairs and her aunt's voice.

"She's up there asleep for chrissakes. Probably just got scared." Aunt Garnet said.

She sounded angry and May knew it was because she had left the company of all the people who turned out to help at husking time. She held her breath waiting to hear what they would say.

"She's young yet," her Grandmother said.

"Dammit, we should've waited until she was asleep."

"She should know what's going on. It's good we came back."

"She's always scared about something. Hell, she gets on my nerves," Garnet said.

"Husking just started," Zea said, "there'll be more nights, people will come back tomorrow."

The furious scraping of a wooden match across a hard surface told May that Aunt Garnet had lit another cigarette.

"I'm going back for a while. No sense in wasting the night here."

Aunt Garnet had closed the door with her last words. The wooden latch snapped hard as the porch door closed and May lifted her head to look out the window. Through the cracked pane she could see a shadow pass below, pass the well beside the house and fade into the dark. She's going over to Tessie Buck's, thought May.

They drank a lot over there and May wondered if Aunt Garnet would come home later. Sometimes she stayed away for days. She remembered her mother had never come back at all. But Zea never said anything about it. If May asked her any questions she would shake her head from side to side and say in Indian, "someday their eyes will open." Then she would make herself busy and at night she would put the lamp in the window.

May was snapped out of her thoughts by the soft glow moving up the stairs. she sat up in bed and watched her own shadow grow longer and more vivid on the wall beside her. Then, Zea's head appeared as she ascended the steps, lamp in hand. It was a slow, painful climb for her. One veiny, large-knuckled hand clutched the rail as the other steadied the lamp, careful to balance the globe. A good one was hard to come by, she would often say, as she cleaned the smoke from its narrow neck. Her Grandmother placed the lamp on the floor at the top of the stairs then came and sat down on the edge of the bed.

"What was it, May?" she asked.

"There was a knock on the door but when I asked who was there no one answered," May said.

Silence.

May continued faster, "I opened the door and looked out but no one was there. It was just dark."

"What did you think it was?"

"I don't know," May said, not lifting her eyes from the bed. She waited.

"You don't want to be scared of the dark," her Grandmother said. "The dark can't hurt you."

"What about when you die? Will it get dark when you die, Grandmother?"

May recoiled from her own words. Her sudden intake of breath caused her to lean back and she looked straight into Zea's face. May absorbed every line in the old face before her as she waited, aching for her reply.

Zea hesitated. Then her Grandmother smiled, crinkling her tired, watery eyes. "I think," she began, "only if we die without noticing the light." She had hugged May with a strong squeeze of her hard, old arms and chuckled. She got up from the bed and chuckled once more as she descended the stairs. May had been puzzled, and she fell asleep thinking of her words over and over.

Now here she was again, at the top of the stairs. She still didn't really understand what her Grandmother had said. But she felt less afraid. Zea and Aunt Garnet were getting ready to go to the longhouse again. She watched the shadows fade on the wall as they moved away from the kitchen door. It was quiet for a few moments then she heard them talking on the porch. They were putting on their jackets, getting ready to leave. Then, her Grandmother's head appeared at the bottom of the stairs.

"Come on, May," she said, "get ready."

Rosalie Jones (Daystar)
dancing "Tales of Old Man," stories of the Blackfoot trickster

"I present material based on Native themes. The stories of creation, animal ancestors, trickster tales, and tribal histories are retold. The new stories are also told; the 20th-century trickster tales of coping with the realities of health, education, and Jim Beam. It is crucial that Native people be a mirror to each other. It is crucial that Native people be *heard and understood* at this time in history, not only for our own survival, but for the survival of the Earth and its people. We are all relatives. I am responsible to my heritage and for its message. Dance is a personal search for expression of those ideas. I have found that dance is how I communicate with myself, as much as with others. I personally feel that all of us, Indian and non-Indian alike, could benefit from Native American philosophy."

Mary Bennett

Cells

Cell, brick, cement, bars, walls, hard,
tv's, soaps, stories, tears, no visitors
allowed, lawyers, liars, guards, big,
touch guns, mean fingers, small bed,
green cloth, disinfectant, toilet, sink,
bars, no window, no door, no knob to turn,
no air, no wind, cold, nightmares, screams,
no touch, no touching.

> I want to touch someone. I want to hold
> that woman who cries every goddamn night.

> I WANT TO TOUCH SOMEONE.

Mary Bennett

My Girlfriend

See, my girlfriend comes to see me sometimes. When they let her in. When they figure I deserve it. She's waiting for me in the visiting room. The guard brings me. She's sitting there so pretty, her black hair tied behind her neck, bushy and wavy across her back, tied with fat red yarn. She's got the sweetest face, smiling at me, that tooth still missing in the front. She holds her hand up to her face, like she wants to hide that missing tooth. She lost it in a fight. Her old man beating her up. She wouldn't take that no more, hit him back, bloodied his nose. She ran away. I found her in a bar. That sweet face, smiling. I took her home. When I close my eyes, I remember the smell of her that first night. She cried. Told me she never been with a woman, why didn't she know it was so good? My girlfriend, when I see her, makes me remember every little thing we did together. Every word we talked. She's waiting for me in the visiting room. Blue shirt with embroidered flowers on the front. She ironed her jeans for me. She stands up, her short, stocky body shaking a little bit. She is beautiful. Her name is Janet. Janet is my girlfriend. I love her. No one else comes to see me here. I try to look my best for Janet. Make sure my hair is combed and braided smooth. I can't wear the cologne I used to wear outside. But Janet doesn't care. We hold hands and sometimes we cry. Her eyes are brown and so deep, I could take a journey in them. And oftentimes I did. She promises to get me out of here, but I know that's impossible. So, my girlfriend comes to see me here. It's too bad. We should be free. Running down the sidewalk. Shouting and laughing. Maybe one day. If they ever want to. But every week, I get to see Janet for one hour. It's good to see her.

Excerpts from Letters

Nov. 9, 1982

Beth greetings,

Very happy you wrote . . .

I'm praying a way will be made for me to get the needed Bond money together. I haven't seen my Son for over a year now. Each second I'm away from him the lonely feelings I endure Becomes worse. I try to remain strong, at times its difficult. When I'm at the lowest, I usually hear from beautiful people such as you.

Cold weather is now here. I missed the entire summer. I was on lock from July 9th till a week and a half ago. They put me on lock for defending a young girl that was being used and abused. They now have me on Closed Custody, thats a little better than what I was on. At least I'm allowed phone calls now. I get 2 hours out of my cell.

I've had plenty of time to really know myself. I meditated a lot, and steadily prayed.

Beth, I do hope we can continue to write each other.

I haven't had much schooling so please excuse any mistakes I made.

(take care) I send much love and prayers to you and yours.

Rita.

December 4, 1982
Saturday

Dear Sister,

Haven't been doing much of anything. Its letters like yours that keep me going.

The days are very long and boring. I don't have a job. The unit I'm in is different from the other four. We stay to ourselves and only go outdoors when they take us. I'm over here on segregation cause I feel I'm unable to cope with all the confusion and going on's in the other units. Its not really all that bad over here. This is also the unit where they have the women come when they break one of the prison rules. But there's six of us staying here cause we choose to.

There's not much to know about me. I was born and raised on a Reservation in North Dakota. A little town by the name of Fort Yates. Its by the Standing Rock Res.

My Dad always worked for the government. He was a Res. police while I was in grade school. My Mom was a housewife and also kept house and took care of this teacher and nurse's children. . . . They were white. When I was about 9 my

93

Mom and Dad divorced. She moved to Aberdeen South Dakota. My Dad went to a custody hearing, she didn't show. So naturally we stayed with him. After a few years my brother and me decided we wanted to spend summers with my Mom so my Dad agreed. She died from Cancer in '73. She was a beautiful woman and I understand why she had to leave us. They fussed and argued all the time, we were unhappy for 2 or 3 years before they divorced. When they divorced their were three of us left at home. My little Brother, myself and one of my Sisters. My Dad worked long hours, we were on our own. I start drinking when I was just about 13 years old. My Grandfather spoiled me, he gave me money daily to support my habit, he had no idea where the money was going. I became involved in a couple breakins. My best friend, my cousin and another kid went to court on the charges. They put me on federal probation, I changed my way of thinking and things got better for me.

I was at my Moms one Summer. I was 14. I met a professional baseball player, much older than I. I became pregnant and was actually happy. When I start to show I couldn't hide it any longer so I talked to my Dad about it. He became angry and said there was no way he was going to allow me to keep my child. I was so hurt, but obeyed my Dad and went to a home for unwed mothers. My baby was put up for adoption against my will. A part of me died. That hurt me more than anything else could have. The Catholics Nuns at the home I went to told me I couldn't see my child at all. So I thought about running from there, but didn't know where to go or who to turn to. My Child was a girl, I caught a glimpse of her, she was so beautiful. My dream was to have a large family.

Then in 1968 when I gave birth to my Son, I was the happiest I've been. We were so close and I would never leave him, only to go to work. I tried having more after him and couldn't. I went to a specialist and he thought I had been fixed when I had my Son. He said I would have to have surgery in order to give birth again. The surgery was so expensive but I thought I could make a way even if I had to work 24 hours a day.

Now that I'm here, I know I'll never have that chance. So now I think about adoption. And I think about my daughter, wonder where she is, if shes okay. And I know one day I'll look for her till I find her.

My precious Son is living with his Father and His Grand-Parents and most of his relations live close by. But I still worry about him, although I know they wouldn't let no one hurt him.

Its been over a year that I've seen him. Right now I'm trying to work out a way for him to come up to visit

Well Beth, I'm gonna let you go for now.

Hope things are going good for you.

Write when you get the feeling. Its always good to hear from you.

Much love and prayers to you and yours.

Rita

Jan. 5, 1983

Dear Beth,

Been wanting to write you sooner, but kept putting it off. I guess I get in those moods where I don't want to do anything but watch T.V.

I wouldn't have known it was christmas if it wasn't for all the advertisements on T.V. But I'm glad it's past, sorta got tired of hearing some of the women crying here. I just looked on it as another day. There's no sense in being depressed, things will change for all of us here. Sooner or later we'll all be free.

Saw my lawyer yesterday. He says he'll bring Derrick (my Son) up to see me. But he's said that before, so I'll believe it when I see him. He says I have a real good chance of a reversal or a new trial.

By the end of March the new building is suppose to be completed. It will be exactly like the one we're in now. Its a shame they couldn't have built it so it wouldn't look so cold. But I guess prisons aren't suppose to look and feel homey.

The building has four sections which are called quads. They refer to them by colors. Brown, Blue, Orange and Yellow. They paint the doors, railings and parts of the walls those colors. I'm in the brown, one of the smaller units. The Blue quad is small too.

The 2 smaller ones have 11 rooms and each has a steel sink and toilet. The shower is on the bottom floor. Glass walls divide the quads. The police sit in a glass cage and control the locking and unlocking of the doors from there. They don't come around us unless their doing count which is once every hour. There made up very simple and cold looking. They give us a metal closet and were allowed our own T.V.s and Radios. My quad has an intercom, cause there usually the units that stay locked down all the time. Having intercoms in each room does no good. The police never answer the calls.

Its about time for me to do my detail. I have to clean the floors in this quad all this week. They'll be calling me in a minute.

Take care my sister. I look forward to your letters. My love and prayers to you.

Rita

Jan. 28, 1983

Dear sister,

Before calling it a day, I thought I'd drop you a few thoughts.

Soon as I get a reply from my Son's Grandmother, my lawyer will know when he'll be able to pick him up to bring him to visit me. I'm really looking forward to that special day. I've waited so long it seems I've waited a lifetime.

I'm very blessed, I've been feeling healthy and at peace with myself. As long as I feel at peace, everyone I come in contact with, I can deal with.

It's getting late, my eyes are becoming heavy. I'm gonna say bye for now. My dreams are a second away. I will walk in freedom till the morning sun.

My prayers and love are with you.

Rita

Dance a Ghost

*(for Mani, murdered with his friend
Marcus outside a phoenix bar)*

Thump   I leap you   shake
            down memories   your black wings
      in my throat   hoarse   You die, are buried
      your name closes the door
                        you reappear at night   eyes wide   I see the uncaught
white man his shoes polished his hand gun
            last pulse   the heart contracts   dreams your knees crumple
      red neon flickers your redman hands   black moccasins on white ground
            curl unseen without frame
No bells on your feet   feathers still   soles
      worn through
         I dance you

Wendy Rose

Sideshow: Julia the Lion Woman
The Ugliest Woman in the World

Soft tanbark, cedar-dark falls
hesitant to your slightest step.
Gray mountains hitch their withers,
lift hay with tusk-guarded trunks;
water sprays beyond guy wires
pegged to and from steel buckets
dented from hoof or tooth or
a dozen generations of small boys.
The men watch arrogantly, the women
tightening their lips and fingering
the beads at their throats; how the men watch
is an unspoken threat the women are hearing
as if from you. Your veil slips
across your wide brown face
flattened from the momentum
of a secret wind, ecru lace and linen
betraying a neanderthal form,
sculpting you back
to an ancient cave, to
the very tops of jungle trees,
and sending you tooth by tooth
to a different beauty than
the click of pennies and dimes.
With manicured fingers
you touch the veil
but do not think it will be
lifted tonight for you remember
the hurried walk dodging stones
among the villagers, how your words
sweet as the yellow canary turned
to bloodsucking lice as they heard them.

You would sing and they would spit
and they would take you to
their killing jar like
an iridescent beetle strayed
from the safe stones in the wilderness.
You pinned them to their deepest fears,
reflecting them from your fish eyes.
You were   a captured cricket,
a rain-bringer, a healer of
abandoned games; you watched other girls
dance cheek to cheek and wiggle free
of the wandering hand
and life danced away from you
like that teased by the promise
to not be alone. Beauty twisted within
and pushed your pain against you
to be nailed like a bronze wolf pelt
on your bones.
They called you the ugliest woman in the world,
the woman with a face like a lion or
an ape, the woman whose long fur swirled
like a shawl around her
in a land where even the wolves
run naked.
I call you
the most beautiful she-wolf,
the highest flying canary,
the most ancient song,
the most faithful magic.
I call you
my mother and my sister
and my daughter and me.

St. John's Indian School, Cheyenne River, South Dakota

Beth Brant

A Long Story

PART ONE: LOSS
dedicated to my Great-Grandmothers
Eliza Powless and Catherine Brant

About 40 Indian children took the train at this depot for the Philadelphia Indian School last Friday. They were accompanied by the government agent, and seemed a bright looking lot.

From *The Northern Observer*
Massena, N.Y. July 20, 1892

I am only beginning to understand what it means for a mother to lose a child.

Anna Demeter, *Legal Kidnapping*

100

1890. . . .

It has been two days since they came and took the children away. My body is greatly chilled. All our blankets have been used to bring me warmth. The women keep the fire blazing. The men sit. They talk among themselves. We are frightened by this sudden child-stealing. We signed papers, the agent said. This gave them rights to take our babies. It is good for them, the agent said. It will make them civilized, the agent said. I do not know civilized. I hold myself tight in fear of flying apart into the air. The others try to feed me. Can they feed a dead woman? I have stopped talking. When my mouth opens, only air escapes. I have used up my sound screaming their names . . . She Sees Deer! Walking Fox! My eyes stare at the room, the walls of scrubbed wood, the floor of dirt. I know there are People here, but I cannot see them. I see a darkness, like the lake at New Moon, black, unmoving. In the center, a picture of my son and daughter being lifted onto the train. My daughter wearing the dark blue, heavy dress. All of the girls dressed alike. Her hair covered by a strange basket tied under her chin. Never have I seen such eyes! They burn into my head even now. My son. His hair cut. Dressed as the white men, his arms and legs covered by cloth that made him sweat. His face, wet with tears. So many children crying, screaming. The sun on our bodies, our heads. The train screeching like a crow, sounding like laughter. Smoke and dirt pumping out of the insides of the train. So many People. So many children. The women, standing as if in prayer, our hands lifted, reaching. The dust sifting down on our palms. Our palms making motions at the sky. Our fingers closing like the claws of the bear. I see this now. The hair of my son is held in my hands. I rub the strands, the heavy braids coming alive as the fire flares and casts a bright light on the black hair. They slip from my fingers and lie coiled and tangled on the ground. I see this. My husband picks up the braids, wraps them in a cloth; takes the pieces of our son away. He walks outside, the eyes of the People on him. I see this. He will find a bottle and drink with the men. Some of the women will join them. They will end the night by singing or crying. It is all the same. I see this. No sounds of children playing games and laughing. Even the dogs have ceased their noises. They lay outside each doorway, waiting. I hear this. The voices of children. They cry. They pray. They call me. . . . Nisten ha. I hear this. Nisten ha.

1978. . . .

I am awakened by the dream. In the dream, my daughter is dead. Her father is returning her body to me in pieces. He keeps her heart. I thought I screamed . . . Patricia! I sit up in bed, swallowing air as if for nourishment. The dream remains in the air. I rise to go to her room. Ellen tries to lead me back to bed, but I have to see once again. I open her door . . . she is gone. The room empty, lonely. They said it was in her best interests. How can it be? She is only six, a baby who needs her mothers. She loves us. This is not happening. I will not believe this. Oh god,

I think I have died. Night after night, Ellen holds me as I shake. Our sobs stifling the air in our room. We lie in our bed and try to give comfort. My mind can't think beyond last week when she left. I would have killed him if I'd had the chance. He took her hand and pulled her to the car. The look in his eyes of triumph. It was a contest to him. I know he will teach her to hate us. He will! I see her dear face. Her face looking out the back window of his car. Her mouth forming the word over and over . . . Mommy Mama. Her dark braids tied with red yarn. Her front teeth missing. Her overalls with the yellow flower on the pocket, embroidered by Ellen's hands. So lovingly she sewed the yellow wool. Patricia waiting quietly until she was finished. Ellen promising to teach her the designs . . . chain stitch, french knot, split stitch. How Patricia told everyone that Ellen made the flower just for her. So proud of her overalls. I open the closet door. Almost everything is gone. A few little things hang there limp, abandoned. I pull a blue dress from a hanger and take it back to my room. Ellen tries to take it away from me, but I hold on, the soft, blue cotton smelling like her. How is it possible to feel such pain and live? Ellen?! She croons my name . . . Mary . . . Mary . . . I love you. She sings me to sleep.

1890. . . .

The agent was here to deliver a letter. I screamed at him and sent curses his way. I threw dirt in his face as he mounted his horse. He thinks I'm a crazy woman and warns me . . . "you better settle down, Annie." What can they do to me? I am a crazy woman. This letter hurts my hand. It is written in their hateful language. It is evil, but there is a message for me. I start the walk up the road to my brother. He works for the whites and understands their meanings. I think about my brother as I pull my shawl closer to my body. It is cold now. Soon there will be snow. The corn has been dried and hangs from our cabin, waiting to be used. The corn never changes. My brother is changed. He says that *I* have changed and bring shame to our clan. He says I should accept the fate. But I do not believe in the fate of child-stealing. There is evil here. There is much wrong in our village. He says I am a crazy woman because I howl at the sky every night. He is a fool! I am calling my children. He says the People are becoming afraid of me because I talk to the air, and laugh like the loon overhead. But I am talking to the children. They need to hear the sound of me. I laugh to cheer them. They cry for us. This paper in my hands has the stink of the agent. It burns my hands. I hurry to my brother. He has taken the sign of the wolf from over the doorway. He pretends to be like those who hate us. He gets more and more like the child-stealers. His eyes move away from mine. He takes the letter from me and begins the reading of it. I am confused. This letter is from two strangers with the names Martha and Daniel. They say they are learning civilized ways. Daniel works in the fields, growing food for the school. Martha cooks and is being taught to sew aprons. She will be going to live with the schoolmaster's wife. She will be a live-in girl. What is live-in girl? I shake my head. The words sound the same to me. I am afraid of Martha and Daniel. These strangers who know my name. My hands and arms are becoming numb. I tear the letters from my brother's fingers. He stares at me, his eyes traitors in his face. He calls after me . . . "Annie . . . Annie." That is not my name! I run back to the road. That is not my name! There is no Martha. There is no Daniel. This is witch work. The paper burns and burns. At my cabin, I quickly dig a hole in the field. The earth is hard and cold, but I dig with my nails. I dig, my hands feeling weaker. I tear the paper and bury the scraps. As the earth drifts and settles, the names Martha and Daniel are covered. I look to the sky and find nothing but endless blue. My eyes are blinded by the color. I begin the howling.

1978. . . .

When I get home from work, there is a letter from Patricia. I make coffee and wait for Ellen, pacing the rooms of our apartment. My back is sore from the line, bending over and down, screwing the handles on the doors of the flashy cars moving by at an incredible pace. My work protects me from questions. The guys making jokes at my expense. Some of them touching my shoulder lightly and briefly, as a sign of understanding. The few women, eyes averted or smiling at me in sympathy. No one talks. There is no time to talk. There is no room to talk, the noise taking up all space and breath. I carry the letter with me as I move from room to room. Finally I sit at the kitchen table, turning the paper around in my hands. Patricia's printing is large and uneven. The stamp has been glued on half-heartedly and is coming loose. Each time a letter arrives, I dread it, even as I long to hear from my child. I hear Ellen's key in the door. She walks into the kitchen, bringing the smell of the hospital with her. She comes toward me, her face set in new lines, her uniform crumpled and stained, her brown hair pulled back in an imitation of a french twist. She knows there is a letter. I kiss her and bring mugs of coffee to the table. We look into each others' eyes. She reaches for my hand, bringing it to her lips. Her hazel eyes are steady in her round face. I open the letter. Dear Mommy. I am fine. Daddy got me a new bike. My big teeth are coming in. We are going to see Grandma for my birthday. Daddy got me new shoes. She doesn't ask about Ellen. I imagine her father standing over her, watching the words painstakingly being printed. Coaxing her. Coaching her. The letter becomes ugly. I frantically tear it in bits and scatter them out the window. The wind scoops the pieces into a tight fist before strewing them in the street. A car drives over the paper, shredding it to mud and garbage. Ellen makes a garbled sound. "I'll leave. If it will make it better, I'll leave." I quickly hold her as the dusk swirls around the room and engulfs us. "Don't leave. Don't leave." I feel her sturdy back shiver against my hands. She begins to kiss my throat and her arms tighten as we move closer. "Ah Mary, I love you so much." As the tears threaten our eyes, the taste of salt is on our lips

103

and tongues. We stare into ourselves, touching our place of pain; reaching past the fear, the guilt, the anger, the loneliness. We go to our room. It is beautiful again. I am seeing it as if with new eyes. The sun is barely there. The colors of cream, brown, green mixing with the wood floor. The rug with its design of wild birds. The black ash basket glowing on the dresser, holding a bouquet of dried flowers, bought at a vendor's stand. I remember the old woman, laughing and speaking rapidly in Polish as she wrapped the blossoms in newspaper. Making a present of her work. Ellen undresses me as I cry. My desire for her breaking through the heartbreak we share. She pulls the covers back, smoothing the white sheets, her hands repeating the gestures done every day at work. She guides me onto the cool material. I watch her remove the uniform of work. An aide to nurses. A healer in spirit. She comes to me full in flesh. My hands are taken with the curves and soft roundness of her. She covers me with the beating of her heart. The rhythm steadies me. Heat is centering me. I am grounded by the peace between us. I smile at her face gleaming above me, round like a moon, her long hair loose and touching my breasts. I take her breast in my hand, bring it to my mouth; suck her as a woman, in desire . . . in faith. Our bodies join. Our hair braids together on the pillow. Brown, black, silver; catching the last face of the sun. We kiss, touch, move to our place of power. Her mouth, moving over my body, stopping at curves and swells of skin, kissing, removing pain. Closer, close, together, woven, my legs are heat, the center of my soul is speaking to her, I am sliding into her, her mouth is medicine, her heart is the earth, we are dancing with flying arms, I shout, I sing, I weep salty liquid, sweet and warm, it coats her throat, this is my life. I love you Ellen, I love you Mary, I love, we love.

1891. . . .

The moon is full. The air is cold. This cold strikes at my flesh as I remove my clothes and set them on fire in the withered corn field. I cut my hair, the knife sawing through the heavy mass. I bring the sharp blade to my arms, legs, and breasts. The blood trickles like small red rivers down my body. I feel nothing. I throw the tangled webs of my hair into the flames. The smell, like a burning animal, fills my nostrils. As the fire stretches to touch the stars, the People come out to watch me . . . the crazy woman. The ice in the air touches me. They caught me as I tried to board the train and search for my babies. The white men tell my husband to watch me. I am dangerous. I laugh and laugh. My husband is only good for tipping bottles and swallowing anger. He looks at me, opening his mouth, and making no sound. His eyes are dead. He wanders from the cabin and looks out at the corn. He whispers our names. He calls after the children. He is a dead man. But I am not! Where have they taken the children? I ask the question of each one who travels the road past our house. The women come and we talk. We ask and ask. They say there is nothing we can do. The white man is a ghost. He slips in and out where we cannot see. Even in our dreams he comes to take away our questions. He works magic that has resisted our medicine. This magic has made us weak. What is the secret about them? Why do they want our babies? They sent the Blackrobes many years ago to teach us new magic. It was evil! They lied and tricked us. They spoke of gods who would forgive us if we became like them. This god is ugly!! He killed our masks. He killed our men. He sends the women screaming at the moon in terror. They want our power. They take our children to remove the inside of them. Our power. It is what makes us Hau de no sau nee. They steal our food, our sacred rattle, the stories, our names. What is left? I am a crazy woman. I look in the fire that consumes my hair and I see their faces. My daughter. My son. They are still crying for me, though the sound grows fainter. The wind picks up their keening and brings it to me. The sound has bored into my brain. I begin howling. At night, I dare not sleep. I fear the dreams. It is too terrible, the things that happen there. In my dream there is wind and blood moving as a stream. Red, dark blood in my dreams. Rushing for our village, the blood moves faster and faster. There are screams of wounded People. Animals are dead, thrown in the blood stream. There is nothing left. Only the air, echoing nothing. Only the earth, soaking up blood, spreading it in the Four Directions, becoming a thing there is no name for. I stand in the field, watching the fire, the People watching me. We are waiting, but the answer is not clear yet. A crazy woman. That is what they call me.

1979. . . .

After taking a morning off work to see my lawyer, I come home, not caring if I call in. Not caring, for once, at the loss in pay. Not caring. My lawyer says there is nothing more we can do. I must wait. As if we have done anything else. He has custody and calls the shots. We must wait and see how long it takes for him to get tired of being mommy and daddy. So . . . I wait. I open the door to Patricia's room. Ellen keeps it dusted and cleaned, in case she will be allowed to visit us. The yellow and bright blue walls are a mockery. I walk to the windows, begin to systematically tear down the curtains. I slowly start to rip the cloth apart. I enjoy hearing the sounds of destruction. Faster and faster, I tear the material into long strips. What won't come apart with my hands, I pull at with my teeth. Looking for more to destroy, I gather the sheets and bedspread in my arms and wildly shred them to pieces. Grunting and sweating, I am pushed by rage and the searing wound in my soul. Like a wolf, caught in a trap, gnawing at her own leg to set herself free, I begin to beat my breasts to deaden the pain inside. A noise gathers in my throat and finds the way out. I begin a scream that turns to howling, then turns to hoarse choking. I want to take my fists, my strong fists, my brown fists, and smash the world until it bleeds. Bleeds! And all the judges in their flapping robes, and the fathers who look for revenge, are ground, ground into dust and disappear with the wind. The word . . . lesbian. Lesbian. The word that makes them panic, makes them afraid, makes them destroy children.   The word that dares them.   Lesbian. *I am one.*   Even for Patricia, even for her, I will not cease to be!   As I kneel amidst the colorful scraps, Raggedy Anns smiling up at me, my chest gives a sigh.   My heart slows to its normal speech.   I feel the blood pumping outward to my veins, carrying nourishment and life.   I strip the room naked.   I close the door.

Lenore Keeshig-Tobias

Mother with Child

Oh Mother, so many times
i would sit on
i would sit on
that kitchen chair

with the night's sleep
or an afternoon of play
tangled in my hair

and you with your
tummy full of child
tummy full of child
would nudge nudge and press

against my shoulders
against my shoulders
against my back

soothing my wildness
while combing my hair
while combing my hair

Denise Panek

For Shirley

who understood the storyteller
and built her hogan far into the woods
while darker spirits whimper and sigh
along the edges of her doorstep

even now, I can feel the pull of her
laughter, still see her hazel eyes disappear
into the folds of her skin as she smiles
still smell the fenugreek, the sweaty
aroma of maple that mingles in her warmth
and in her breath

Cedar Woman, loving the Indian child
before it was fashionable, sometimes I
can see you rise and escape through the cracks
in the timbers, resting in the trees
counting the thunderclouds

Cedar Woman, I rejoice in your raindance
the Winds lean forth to hear you.

Ina, 1979

Nameless one—
Hastily, called "Butte Woman"
Paha win
By the keeper of the
White Buffalo Calf Woman's Pipe.

A woman of many names,
all kinship designations—
Tuwin—aunt
Oonchi—grandmother
Cuwe—older sister
Hankashi—female cousin
Ina—mother
all honorable,
all good.

I prefer
Napewakanwin
"Sacred Hands Woman"
Suggested by our own *wapiya*
the healer.
But refused by you
as being too honoring.

The *wapiya* now insists
that you were given the name
Wapahaluta win
"RedWarbonnet Woman"
when you were a child.

But nameless one, in Lakota,
Your deeds live on and are
recounted.

109

I knew that you would remain
for Christmas—a Christian celebration
A time you enjoyed,
A festivity,
A ritual.
"The more the merrier,"
You always said
about the houseful of *tiospaye* members.
An extended family of drunks,
free-loaders,
homeless ones,
arrogant ones,
lazy ones.

January was a worry for me, too.
It must have been for you.
You often said,
"If I make it through January . . ."
Moon of Cracking Limbs,
of trees,
of people,
of thoughts.

But you called this moon
"When the door is blocked."
Snow, fine and dry,
blowing, swirling, stacking
against the tipi flap,
now the wooden door
of the log cabin.

I recall your concern for others.
"I'd rather not die
in winter time . . .
It's too hard
for the grave-diggers."

I knew.
It would be more rewarding
to start the final journey
atop a scaffold—looking upward
toward the "spirit trail"
the Milky Way.

The "Spirit Trail"
is bright and smoothly shining
in the "moon of Black Cherries"
or
"When the Tree Limbs Crack."

It seems more brilliant
in January.
He waits.
Sitting Crow has brightened the trail
for your failing eyes.
And the sun has "built fires
around himself,"
to keep you warm
on your travel.

Kateri Sardella

Urban Dwellers

1

The alley is lit occasionally with 60-watt bulbs that hang nakedly in narrow door-ways. There is garbage in garbage cans and garbage in piles on the curbs.

Wheeler's is the name of the fruit and vegetable stand on the boulevard that closes at 9 p.m. on summer nights. At 9:15, the employees bring out the produce that didn't sell, and won't sell the following day because it has started the visible signs of decay. They dump it in the alley in wooden crates, beneath one of the bare bulbs. They leave it there for the rats or the garbage collector, whichever comes first.

There are two small children in the alley tonight. They sit on the curb where no light hits and wait for the help to go home. Their stomachs gurgle and their mouths water. They have not eaten yet today.

David and Jessie both have two brown paper bags, one tucked inside the other, to hold whatever they will be able to find to take home tonight.

At 9:25, they stand, stretch, and walk quietly to the decomposing pile of food.

"God, David, look at all this stuff! We got enough here for tonight and tomorrow. Look at this watermelon. It's really only got a couple of bad spots and it's almost a whole thing!

"Come on, Jess, let's hurry up. Here, put these potatoes in your bag. I'll carry the watermelon."

"Hey, look! Canteloupe! Wow, David. There's a lot of good stuff here!" Jessie ignored the mashed-in gooey part and put the canteloupe in the bag.

"Sh! I think I hear something!" David pushed Jessie down behind a smelly box of lettuce and jumped down behind her. Down the alley, they heard someone walking. As the steps grew louder, they could tell the man was staggering. "Ya hear that? I think he's drunk," David whispered. Jessie giggled and the man crashed into a pile of broccoli and eggplant. He grabbed at the air as he pulled himself to his feet. As he passed the children's hiding place, he kicked the box of lettuce before he headed out of the alley.

"Let's hurry up and get out of here, David. I'm getting scared!"

"Okay. You grab those peaches. I got the watermelon. Let's go!"

"Geez, I'm hungry. Hey! Look! Oranges!"

"Oh God, Jessie, they stink!"

Jessie picked up one of the rotting oranges and flung it in the direction the old drunk had gone in. Then she picked up her sack and hugged the food to her body as she followed her brother out of the alley.

112

It was a three-mile walk home. The streets were quiet once the children left the boulevard. When they passed the train station and walked under the bridge, they threw some of the worst parts of their food up at the pigeons.

"David, remember when Dad worked under here?"

"Yeah, and do you remember how bad he stunk when he did?" David burst out laughing and Jessie joined in, once she heard his amplified voice bounce off the steel and cement. "Hey Jessie, remember when Dad took us to the fair? Boy, he saved a lot of money for that!"

"Did it cost a lot?"

"It sure did. Remember the races? Remember that one car that got on fire? Wasn't that something! We had a great time, didn't we!"

Jessie didn't know whether she liked talking about their father or not. It always ended up making her sad. Every time she came this way, she remembered when she brought the baby here to see their father at his lunch break. A butterfly landed on Bobby's shoulder and when she told her mother about it, she said it was a sign of good luck. Now, Bobby's belly was swollen and all he did was sleep, wake up and cry, and fall back to sleep again. "Yeah, I remember. We had a lot of good times, didn't we, David? Huh, David?"

3

The room that should have been a living room was in a shambles. There was an old worn twin mattress lying in the middle of the room. A dirty blue cotton blanket and a dingy white pillowcase filled with rags were strewn across the bed. The baby lay there; his legs were tucked up to his chest and his face was frozen in a grimace of some unknown pain. Jessie sat at the edge of the mattress and watched as Bobby crammed his little blue fist into his mouth and sucked on it. She watched the blue swollen vein in his neck and knew that at any moment it would burst and the baby's head would blow off. The fear in her belly rose and as it did, she wondered how it would feel to die. Would it hurt? She was sure it would hurt her little brother. She sat there and wished that she could wish that she would die. She didn't know why, but she wanted to live. She wanted to live until she was old and she wanted to live all her life.

David should have been back by now. Where did he go, anyway? What if he didn't come back? What if the cops got him and she would never see him again? Where did they take him? Where should she look? Bobby was falling asleep and Ronnie had already been sleeping a long time now. How could they sleep when their oldest brother was out there, somewhere, and probably never coming home again? What should she do? What would happen to them if David never came home again?

4

The night air was cool, but Jessie's skin was clammy and prickly. The streetlights shone bright. She could see the length of the block but David was nowhere in sight. She wanted to scream to him. As she ran the length of the block, she took quick glances between the buildings just in case he was lying in one of the alleyways, dead with a bullet in his head or a knife sticking out of his chest.

There was a young white couple sitting on the stoop of their apartment building. Jessie saw them through a heart-pounding haze. Were they laughing? Were they staring at her, at her clothes, at the fear in her eyes? Did they have her brother locked up in their apartment? Did they hate Indians and did they take the hair from his scalp and hang it on their clothesline to dry? She knew there were people like that.

They were drinking wine. They were drinking wine and they were no-good-drunks! Jessie forced herself to walk, not run by them. She stole glances at them. They weren't paying any attention to her. She saw into the lit entrance of the apartment building and knew David wasn't in there.

She felt her weak knees start into a run. She ran another block and then she saw him. He was on the corner in front of the drugstore and he was talking with another boy. Why was he doing that? Why wasn't he home? Why was he just standing there talking with another boy? Why wasn't he home and why hadn't he taken her with him?

She fell into a walk. David saw her and waved his arm to her. He turned to the other boy for a second, turned back to her, and came jogging across the street. "Hi. What are you doing out? I told you to stay with the kids, Jess. Is something wrong?"

"No. I got bored. They're sleeping and I didn't have nothing to do. You comin' home now?"

"Yeah. Look what I got. You want one?" Out of his pants pocket, David pulled two cigarettes. He lit one, took a puff, and handed it to her. Jessie took a long drag on it, felt it burn her lungs, and coughed out the smoke. David said, "Good, huh?"

"Yeah," she said. "Where did you get 'em?"

"From that kid you saw me with. I know him from when we lived on Catherine Street. I told him we were just visiting. I told him we came down from the island."

"Why did you tell him that?"

"So no one will find out where we are. I went looking for Mom tonight."

"Did ya see her?"

"No. No one has. But don't worry; she's okay."

"How do you know that? Maybe she's in jail."

"No, she's not. She's around somewhere. She's okay. Come on. Let's go home." David threw the cigarette onto the sidewalk and stomped on it with his sneaker.

5

David saw their mother that night. That boy didn't give him any cigarettes. She did. She told him that he was practically a man. And she gave him four Pall Malls. He smoked one of them in front of her while they stood on the sidewalk in front of the bar. She told him that she would be home tonight. She said that it was a nice warm night and she felt like visiting with the people in the bar. She said that Tom was a real nice man and he didn't know that she had kids, so David shouldn't go in the bar with her; but if he came in and went to the back room where the pool table was, she'd get him a Coca-Cola before he went home.

David did go to the back of the bar and went into the men's room. He came out and watched two old drunks argue about where to put the black ball, and waited for his mother. He waited for half an hour before he knew for sure that she wasn't coming back there and she wasn't going to buy him a Coca-Cola. As he walked through the bar and onto the sidewalk, he didn't look for her. He knew that she had left as soon as he entered the back room.

When David and Jessie got back to the flat, they climbed through the kitchen window. David lit a match so that they could see their way to the living room.

Bobby had rolled off the mattress and was curled up on the floor. Ronnie lay on his back and his fingers were moving like he was dreaming about fiddling with a toy or something. David picked up the baby and laid him next to his other brother. Then David got down on the mattress too.

"Jessie, you can get in the middle. Come on."

"Thanks, David," Jessie said as she squeezed in between David and Bobby. "David, I'm scared. When do you think Mom will come home? I mean, I know you don't know, but do you think we'll find her?"

"You know we will, Jess. It's okay. She'll be home."

They both lay there stretched out like two slivers on a board. David reached out and hugged all three of them to him. Jessie fell asleep and David lay there thinking. Why didn't she tell him to just go home? Why did she have to lie to him? Why didn't she just say she wasn't coming home; then he wouldn't have to stay awake and wait for her every night.

6

Days turned into weeks. Twice, David found his mother. Twice, she told him that she would be home that night. She didn't ask if they were hungry. She didn't say that she missed them. Didn't ask how they were doing. Each time, she said the weather was beautiful and she'd be home tonight.

On the second Tuesday in June, the Wonder Bread Man was going to be at the supermarket in their neighborhood. The Wonder Bread truck would pull up to the curb outside the store and out of its little side door would emerge a man dressed all in white, walking on stilts that made him look nine feet tall. And he would pass out little tiny loaves of white bread to the children that gathered to see him.

David was there early. He hid a brown grocery bag behind the building and stood around like he didn't even know the Wonder Bread Man was coming. All the kids, including his sister, Jessie, were running in and out of the store asking the clerks when the man was supposed to be there.

He came and left within twenty minutes. Jessie was so amazed at the sight of him that she forgot to save the little loaves of bread. She had taken four packages from him and stuffed her face with the fresh doughy bread. David made numerous trips behind the store and when it was time to go home, he had enough for all four of them for at least three days.

7

David took the discarded milk bottle out of the garbage on Green Street and headed down the hill towards the playground. It was the school playground where they used to go every day. Now that it was no longer in session, he could pass the school without any fear of being caught by the truant officer. The water fountain was still turned on.

David filled his milk bottle with the cold water and headed back up the hill to their flat.

Bobby was lying naked on the mattress. His bottom was caked with greenish yellow excrement and flies buzzed about his body.

David took a rag out of the filthy pillowcase and poured some of the water from the bottle on it. As he wiped his little brother's bottom, the baby screamed and his rear end glowed bright red.

Then, David took the soiled diaper out of the back door, poured the rest of the water on it, slapped it against the tree a few times and then hung it on a low-hanging branch. The sun shone bright and the diaper would be dry within a couple hours.

8

"Hey, Kid! Come here. I wanna talk ta ya. Where's your goddamned mother? That no good son ofa bitchin' rotten Indian! You tell her I want my money! You hear me, you little bastard? You see that little bastard run, John? He better run! He was probably in here to steal from me!

"Aw, come on, Dan, he's just a kid. Why do ya always have to talk to him like that, huh? His father is a paizan, you know that."

"His father was a paizan, John. Not no more. He's dead, don't ya remember? And it's because he married that goddamned no good for nothin' Injun lady! So

116

what do you want, anyway? And don't ask me for no White Owl. That son of a bitch hasn't showed up yet. That bastard! He try'n to ruin my business, I know it!"

9

David sat on the curb. His stomach hurt. His head ached and he missed his mother and father. He missed a lot of things. And he didn't want to take care of everything all the time but he had to. From here he'd walk over to the south end. Some guy that hung out at Lou's would probably have seen David's mother.

And he'd tell him the truth. That guy would tell David where his mother was because, David knew, that guy really liked his mother. And that guy never really lied to David before about anything. That guy was always giving Mom some money and telling her to go buy her kids some food. And she'd tell him, sure thing.

A cop car drove by and David put down his head. The cop didn't do nothing. Just kept going, and David didn't know what to feel about it.

10

"Hey David, what's the matter? Come on, get up." Jessie pushed on his shoulder. "Come on, get up! You're scarin' me!" She punched his shoulder again. He just lay there. "David! David! Get up! You fuckin' bastard, get up! David! David, you fucker! You fucker! I hate you!"

He just lay there. His eyes stayed closed. His skin tingled where his little sister punched him. All Mom had to do was come home. That's all. Then everything would be alright again. He hated her. But he loved her so much and he didn't know what to do. Everything was falling apart. What were they going to do?

EPILOGUE

Mom came home, finally. But not for long. Really, just long enough to get us a new place to stay. And we stayed there for a while but then I ended up here. And David ended up in another place and so did Bobby and Ronnie.

Nuns take care of me here. And they feed us all the time. But they also hit me and tell me that it's good for me. They say, if I don't watch out, I'll turn out just like Mom. I guess they're right. They should know, being since they're so close to God and everything.

One nun tells me to scrub myself real hard when I take a shower; which I do every day. She says that I'm not really this dark, that it will wash off if I shower good and behave myself.

It's not really hard to behave here. There's nothing to do and I don't have to go out at night anymore. I miss my brothers though. I asked the nun when I would see them again and she said there was no need to, since we're all happy now. I guess she's right. I don't know.

THE MOTHER

© JAUNE QUICK-N-SEE SMITH 1984

The young warrior

The young warrior,
Seeing the world through brand-new eyes,
Brought up thinking she was special and good.

Lakota people can be proud again.

When an injustice is done to one of "the people,"
The warriors gather.

The woman warrior is among them,
Proud and strong,
Because she is a fighter.

The words flow off the tongues of the new orators,
Telling of the old ways,
And why being Indian is worth fighting for,
Mesmerized by the sense of strength and duty,
To become a warrior and keep the Lakota ways alive.

Tradition as told by men,
Written in history books by white men,
Religion didn't escape their influence.

Despite being told the women's squad is assigned the kitchen,
She guards the rooms and buildings from passing racists.

While the Lakota people make their stand,
Quiet defiance to the men who say, "respect your brother's vision,"
She mutters, "respect your sister's vision too."

She supported you in Wounded Knee,
She was with you at Sioux Falls,
Custer,
And Sturgis,
And has always remembered you,
Her Indian people,
In her prayers.

She has listened to women who were beaten by the men they love,
Or their husbands,
And gave strength to women who were raped,
As has the Sacred Mother Earth.

At some point asking where Tradition for women was being decided.

As a Traditional Lakota woman you are asked to approach a relative
or your spouse to speak your thoughts and feelings at a public meeting,
Not to touch a feather, or not to handle food at what the white culture
once referred to as the "sick time."

Woman warrior once told to break the stereotype of the white people,
She is also told to walk ten steps behind a man.

The new eyes that once were in awe at what the world had to offer,
Looks down at this new girl child,
The Lakota woman warrior knows her daughter also has a vision.

Nan Benally

Navaho Sings

Here I am
　　freezing and being blinded
　　　　by the smoke from the nearby fire.
The night is clear
　　where I can feel the chill
　　　　all throughout my body.
That's why I take the lesser of the two evils.
　　Stand in the smoke
　　　　And stay warm.
My sister is still trying to give me
　　final reminders, and as I listen,
I wonder how I ever got myself into
　　　　this predicament.

Nervous and scared
　　　　I wait
　　as all the others are waiting.
　　　　There are others
　　　　　　who have already begun dancing.
I watch them intently
　　hoping to rehearse in my mind
　　　　what I'm supposed to do.
Finally, it is our turn.
　　My sister glances at me
　　　　one last time as we form our lines.
I smile at her
　　and I hope that I won't
　　　　fall or trip
If I can get through this
　　it will be something
　　　　short of a miracle.

We begin the ritual
of gathering out sprigs
and forming our lines.
My father begins and
we all follow suit.

The singing came easy
but I remember
little else.
Everything
becomes one.
The sky,
the chill,
the faces,
the ground.

Lenore Keeshig-Tobias

(a found poem)

CHAPTER 149

An Act Respecting Indians

Section 11. Subject to section 12,
a person is entitled to
to be registered, if that
that person (c) is a male who
who is a direct descendent in
in the male line of a male
male person described in
in paragraph (a) or (b);

Section 11. Subject to section 12,

a person is entitled to
to be registered, if that
that person (f) is the wife or
or widow of a person who is
is registered by virtue of paragraph
paragraph (a), (b), (c), (d) or (e);

Section 12 (1) (b)

The following persons are not
not allowed to be registered
registered namely, (b) a woman who married
married a person who is not an Indian,
Indian, unless that woman is subsequently
subsequently the wife or widow of a person
person described in section 11.

CHAPTER 149

AN ACT RESPECTING INDIANS

123

CHAPTER 149

(subsequently and
without reservation)

Fathers brothers uncles
chiefs warriors politicians
Where are the Women

"out there" you point
"somewhere"

we reach out into the mist
to women you refuse to see
to strength you cannot give

and will not give to emotion
you cannot feel to the other
half of our beginnings

we have ourselves and our daughters
and you my fathers have
sons and sons and sons

and section 12 (1) (b)
in the Act Respecting Indians

Marilou Awiakta

Amazons in Appalachia

According to Albert Einstein, there is a dimension beyond time/space where time stands still—past, present and future are one. My Cherokee ancestors knew how to enter this dimension at will. Since their spirits abide in my native mountains in East Tennessee, I walk with the strong, nurturing grandmothers that Timberlake met on his journey.

"Where are your women?"

The speaker is Attakullakulla, a Cherokee chief renowned for his shrewd and effective diplomacy. He has come to negotiate a treaty with the whites. Among his delegation are women "as famous in war as powerful in the Council." Their presence also has ceremonial significance: it is meant to show honor to the other delegation. But that delegation is composed of males only. To them the absence of their women is irrelevant, a trivial consideration.

To the Cherokee, however, reverence for women/Mother Earth/life/spirit is interconnected. Irreverence for one is likely to mean irreverence for all. Implicit in their chief's question, "Where are your women?" the Cherokee hear, "Where is your balance? What is your intent?" They see that the balance is absent and are wary of the white men's motives. They intuit the mentality of destruction.

I turn to my own time (1983). I look at the Congress, the Joint Chiefs of Staff, the Nuclear Regulatory Commission . . . at the hierarchies of my church, my university, my city, my children's school. "Where are your women?" I ask.

Wary and fearful, I call aside one of Attakullakulla's delegation. I choose her for the gray streak of experience in her hair, for her staunch hips and for the lively light in her eyes that indicates an alert, indomitable spirit. "Grandmother, I need your courage. Sing to me about your life."

Her voice has the clear, honing timbre of the mountains.

I am Cherokee.

My people believe in the Spirit that unites all things.

I am woman. I am life force. My word has great value.

The man reveres me as he reveres Mother Earth and his own spirit.

The Beloved Woman is one of our principal chiefs. Through her the Spirit often speaks to the people. In the Great Council at the capital she is a powerful voice. Concerning the fate of hostages, her word is absolute.

Women share in all of life. We lead sacred dances. In the Council we debate freely with men until an agreement is reached. When the nation considers war, we have a say, for we bear the warriors.

Sometimes I go into battle. I also plant and harvest.

I carry my own name and the name of my clan. If I accept a mate, he and our children take the name of my clan. If there is deep trouble between us, I am as free to tell him to go as he is to leave. Our children and our dwelling stay with me. As long as I am treated with dignity, I am steadfast.

> I love and work and sing.
> I listen to the Spirit.
> In all things I speak my mind.
> I walk without fear.
> I am Cherokee.

I feel the Grandmother's power. She sings of harmony, not dominance. And her song rises from a culture that repeats the wise balance of nature: the gender capable of bearing life is not separated from the power to sustain it. *A simple principle. Yet, in spite—or perhaps because—of our vast progress in science and technology, the American culture where I live has not grasped this principle. In my county alone there are 2600 men who refuse to pay child support, leaving their women and children with a hollow name, bereft of economic means and sometimes even of a safe dwelling. On the national level, the U.S. Constitution still does not include equal rights for women.*

The Grandmother can see this dimension of time/space as well as I—its imbalance, its irreverence, its sparse presence of women in positions of influence. And she can hear the brave women who sing for harmony and for transforming power. "My own voice is small, Grandmother, and I'm afraid. You live in a culture that believes in your song. How can you understand what women of my time have to cope with?"

Grasping my chin gently, the Grandmother turns my face back toward the treaty council. "Listen to Attakullakulla's question again. When he says, 'Where are your women?' look into the eyes of the white delegation and you will see what I saw."

On the surface, hardness—the hardness of mind split from spirit, the eyes of conquerors. Beyond the surface, stretching future decades deep, are crumpled treaties. Rich farms laid waste. And, finally, the Cherokee, goaded by soldiers along a snowbound trail toward Oklahoma—a seemingly endless line of women, men and children, wrapped in coats and blankets, their backs bowed against the cold. In the only gesture of disdain left to them, they refuse to look their captors in the face.

Putting my arms around the Grandmother, I lay my head on her shoulder. Through touch we exchange sorrow, despair that anything really changes. I'm ashamed that I've shown so little courage. She is sympathetic. But from the pressure of her arms I also feel the stern, beautiful power that flows from all the Grandmothers, as it flows from our mountains themselves. It says, "Dry your tears. Get up. Do for yourself or do without. Work for the day to come. Be joyful."

"Joyful, Grandmother?!" I draw away. "Sorrow, yes. Work, yes. We must work . . . up to the end. But such a hardness is bearing down on my people. Already soldiers are gathering. Snow has begun to fall. This time we will walk the Trail of Fire. With the power of the atom, they can make the world's people walk it. How can you speak of joy?"

"Because, for those who die, death is death. A Trail of Tears for the Cherokee, a Trail of Fire for all—it is the same. But without joy, there is no hope. Without hope, the People have no chance to survive. Women know how to keep hope alive . . . at least, some women do."

The reproach stings and angers me . . . because she is right. My joy, my hope are lost. I don't know how to find them again. Silently, my thoughts flow toward her. Hers flow back to me, strong, without anger.

"Come," she says.

"Where?"

"To Chota—the capital—to see the Beloved Woman."

I've heard of her—Nanyehi . . . "spirit person/immortal." Nanyehi, whom the whites call Nancy Ward and hold in great respect . . . the Beloved Woman whose advice and counsel are revered throughout the Cherokee nation. She is said to have a "queenly and commanding presence," as well as remarkable beauty, with skin the color and texture of the wild rose.

Not ready . . . I'm not ready for this. Following the Grandmother along the forest trail, I sometimes walk close, sometimes lag behind. Puny—that's what I am. Puny, puny, puny—the worst charge that can be leveled at any mountain woman, red or white. It carries pity, contempt, reproach. When we meet, the Beloved Woman will see straight into my spirit. I dread to feel the word in her look.

I know about her courage. She works ceaselessly for harmony with white settlers, interpreting the ways of each people to the other. From her uncle and mentor, Attakullakulla, she has learned diplomacy and the realities of power. She understands that the Cherokee ultimately will be outnumbered and that war will bring sure extinction. She counsels them to channel their energies from fighting into more effective government and better food production (she also introduces them to dairying). To avoid bloodshed, she often risks censure and misunderstanding to warn either side of an impending attack, then urges resolution by arbitration. In the councils she speaks powerfully on two major themes: "Work for peace. Do not sell your land."

All the while, she knows the odds . . .

As the Grandmother and I pass through my hometown of Oak Ridge, I look at the nest of nuclear reactors there and weigh the odds of survival—for all people. The odds are small. But not impossible. My own song for harmony and reverence with the atom is a small breath. But it may combine with others to make a warm and mighty wind, powerful enough to transform the hardness and cold into life. It is not impossible.

I walk closer to the Grandmother. In this timeless dimension, we could move more rapidly, but she paces my spirit, holding it to a thoughtful rhythm as we cross several ridges and go down into the Tellico Valley. We walk beside the quiet, swift waters of the Little Tennessee River. Chota is not far off.

What time/space will the Grandmother choose for me to meet the Beloved Woman? I imagine a collage of possibilities:

1775/Nanyehi fights beside her husband in a battle against the Creeks. When he is killed, she takes his rifle and leads the Cherokee to victory. Afterwards, warriors sing of her deeds at Chota and the women and men of the Great Council award her the high office she will hold for more than half a century. She is seventeen, the mother of a son and a daughter.

1776/Having captured the white woman, Mrs. Lydia Bean, Cherokee warriors tie her to the stake. Just as they light the fire, Nanyehi arrives on the scene, crying, "No woman will be burned at the stake while I am Beloved Woman!" Her word is absolute. Mrs. Bean goes free.

1781/At the Long Island Treaty Council, Nanyehi is the featured speaker. "Our cry is for peace; let it continue. . . . This peace must last forever. Let your women's sons be ours; our sons be yours. Let your women hear our words." (*Note:* no white women are present.)

Colonel William Christian responds to her. "Mother: We have listened well to your talk. . . . No man can hear it without being moved by it. . . . Our women shall hear your words. . . . We will not meddle with your people if they will be still and quiet at home and let us live in peace."[1]

Although the majority of Cherokee and whites hold the peace, violence and bloodshed continue among dissenting factions.

1785/The Hopewell Treaty Council convenes in South Carolina. Attending the Council are four commissioners appointed by Congress, thirty-six Chiefs and about a thousand Cherokee delegates. Again, the Beloved Woman speaks eloquently. Knowing full well the pattern of strife that precedes this Council, she bases her talk on positive developments. "I take you by the hand in real friendship . . . I look on you and the red people as my children. Your having determined on peace is most pleasant to me, for I have seen much trouble during the late war. . . . We are now under the protection of Congress and shall have no more disturbance. The talk I have given you is from the young warriors I have raised in my town, as well as myself. They rejoice that we have peace, and hope the chain of friendship will never more be broken."[2]

Hope—that quality so necessary for survival. The Beloved Woman never loses hope. Perhaps I will learn the source of her strength by sharing her private moments: I may see her bend in joy over her newborn second daughter (fathered by the white trader Bryant Ward, to whom she is briefly married in the late 1750s) or hear her laugh among her grandchildren and the many orphans to whom she gives a home. Or, I may stand beside her in 1817 as she composes her last message to her people. Too ill at age seventy-nine to attend the Council, she sends the last message by her son. Twenty years before it begins, she sees the Trail of Tears loom ahead and her words have one theme: "My children, do not sell your land."

Nanyehi . . . Nancy Ward . . . "as famous in war as powerful in the Council."

The Grandmother's hand on my arm halts my imaginings. We stand at the edge of a secluded clearing, rimmed with tall pines. In the center is a large log house and around it women—many women—move through sun and shadow. Some walk in the clearing. Others cluster on the porch, talking quietly, or sit at the edge of the forest in meditation. Not far from us, a woman who is combing another's hair leans forward to whisper and their laughter rises into the soughing pines.

A great weaving is going on here, a deep bonding . . .

"This is the menstrual lodge," says the Grandmother. "When our power sign is with us we come here. It is a sacred time—a time for rest and meditation. No one is allowed to disturb our harmony. No warrier may even cross our path. In the menstrual lodge many things are known, many plans are made . . ."

"And the Beloved Woman?"

"She is here."

"What year is this, Grandmother?"

"It is not a year; it is a *season*—you and the Beloved Woman are meeting when each of you is in her forty-seventh season." From the expression on my face the Grandmother knows I appreciate the wisdom of her choice: Four and seven are the sacred numbers of the Cherokee; four symbolizing the balance of the four directions. It is the season when no women should or can afford to be "puny." The Grandmother nods. Motioning me to wait, she goes toward the lodge, threading her way through the women with a smile of recognition here, the touch of outstretched fingers there.

With my hands behind my hips, I lean against the stout, wiry-haired trunk of a pine. Its resinous scent clears my mind. These women are not the Amazons of the Greek fable. While they are independent and self-defined, they do not hate men and use them only at random for procreation. They do not elevate their daughters, or kill, cripple, or make servants of their sons. But did the Greek patriarchs tell the truth? If Attakullakulla had asked them, "Where are *your* women?" they would have answered with a shrug. I'm wary of the Greeks bearing fables. Although there is little proof that they described the Amazons accurately, ample evidence suggests that they encountered—and resented—strong women like my Grandmothers and characterized them as heinous in order to justify destroying them (a strategy modern patriarchs still use).

In any case, why should I bother with distant Greeks and their nebulous fables when I have the spirits of the Grandmothers, whose roots are struck deep in my native soil and whose strength is as tangible and tenacious as the amber-pitched pine at my back.

Like the husk of a seed, my Western education/conditioning splits and my spirit sends up a green shoot. With it comes a long-buried memory: I am twelve years old. Mother has told me that soon I will be capable of bearing life. "Think of it, Marilou. It's a sacred power, a great responsibility." I think . . . and wait for the power sign. It comes. Mother announces to my father, "Our little girl is a woman now . . ." He smiles. "Well . . . mighty fine." In the evening we have a dinner in my honor. Steam from corn on the cob, fried chicken, green beans and cornbread mingles in my mind with the private odor, warm and pungent, that Mother describes as "fresh" (the rural term for mammals in season). I feel wholesome, proud, in harmony with the natural order.

I am ready now to meet the Beloved Woman . . .

"What was it like," you ask, "to be in her presence?"
"Come. I will show you." It is midnight/June/the full moon. Behind a farmhouse near the Kentucky border, you and I walk barefoot through the coarse grass. Crickets and treefrogs are drowsy. Birds are quiet. And we are enveloped in a powerful, sweet odor that transforms the night. Too pungent to be honeysuckle. Too fecund for roses. It recalls a baby's breath just after nursing, along with the memory of something warm and private that lingers at the edge of the mind . . .
Sniffing the air, we seek the source — and find it. The cornfield in bloom. Row on row of sturdy stalks, with their tassels held up to the moon. Silently, in slow rhythm, we make our way into the field. The faint rustle of growing plants flows around and through us, until, when we stop by a tall stalk, there seems no division between flesh and green. We rub the smooth, sinewy leaves on our cheeks and touch a nubile ear, where each grain of pollen that falls from the tassel will make a kernel, strong and turgid with milk. Linking arms around the stalk, we lift our faces to the drifting pollen and breathe the spirit of the Corn Woman — the powerful, joyous, nurturing odor of one complete-in-herself.

"Where are your women?"
We are here.

---

1. Ilene J. Cornwell, "Nancy Ward," *Heroes of Tennessee,* Memphis State University Press (Memphis, 1979), 41.

2. Pat Alderman, *Nancy Ward,* The Overmountain Press (Johnson City, Tennessee, 1978), 69.

Nila NorthSun

Pow Wow Pictures

Vickie Sears

Pow Wow

There are cool breezes
    in
        warm spring sunslants
           tapping
      the dancers bells
      and
          freeflowing feathers
             rhythmically dipping
    with
      weaving bodies.
There are spirit songs
    beating the
      drums.
          heyya heyya heyya
            rises from the throats of
    circled
      groundsitting singers.
         dancers
           feel their circle
    around
      drumsinging.
There are children
    everywhere
      running
        laughing
   wandering freely
    to explore
        because that is how we grow.

There are eyes that speak
        most of all you need
            to understand
                and
                    teasing
        from behind blackorb grins
            to keep you
                humbly human
                    giving
        smiles at your own foolishness.
There are afternoon and evening fires
        of fry bread
            beans
                    meat
                        and beer.
        everyone has a plate
            yet
                    takes from others.
                        children sodapop pass
        without asking
            if
                    they should share.
                        things are good.
        people recognize themselves
            as
                    ONE
                        of the earth circle.
        sing
I am the universe
        as made by the
            Great Spirit.
                    ga lv la di   ga dv gi a   a qua dnv do
                    (heaven   hear my   heart)

am a living circle
   as
      the drums tell it.
      am sun
as the drums shine it.
   am sky
      as the drums fly it.
      and
I dance it
   sure
      softly
      strongly
prayerfully
   circle
      on
      circle
spirit-healing circles.
   for that time
      our culture
   needs
      no explanation.
      no missionary speaks of
      heathen faith.
   efforts to
      make us
      assimilate
      are
      worthy only of a joke.
      for the length of drumming
      all is
whole
   as it should be.
      everyone is
      full
circle on circle
   dancing
      the song
      of
      living.

Nila NorthSun

the 49

"my one & only
although you're with
another one
dear
it's always only you
i am thinking of

someday our dream
will come true
& then you'll always
be mine
be mine from
now until eternity"

hey ah hey
under pendleton blankets
or dance shawls
huddled by a drum
bouncing to the rhythm
of the 49
it feels so good
shivering in the starlight
passing beers
singing loud
& rocking
to the 49

Nora Naranjo-Morse

Oklahoma Rt 66

Too many tumbleweeds on 66
    Talking about finding Oklahoma
    Talk about Pow-Wows
    And that Navajo with braids
        EE-Yah!

Passed Amarillo
    And Diane said skins were lost
    And I agreed
    And I agreed

The tumbleweeds ended on the boulevard
    Right up to the Sunset Bar
    After the Pow-Wow
    After the Navajo
        EE-Yah!
        EE-Yah!

Nora Noranjo-Morse

Witchcraft

Changing foot prints
Coyote witchcraft
And the Pueblo woman leaving the aspens

Witchcraft Woman

It was you that black nite
You looking in my window
Making me think you were a dream

Anna Lee Walters

The Devil and Sister Lena

Lena was a religious woman. She attended church at every opportunity even though an ancient tribal belief had been deeply instilled in her. She did not forsake "the old way" as she called it, and she taught both ways to the grandchild in her care. From the time it was a baby, she carried it not only to a variety of churches, but to the "Indian doings" as well. The churches dotted the hills and Lena knew each church that sat near her family's alloted land. She had lived there for three-quarters of a century, her life-time.

Lena's faith in all the denominations baffled and angered each pastor of the the little country church-houses. She was not the only one like that, there were other Indian people who were the same. The ministers decided then that the Indian flock were like children who had simple minds and led simple lives. Painstakingly, theology was explained to each of these potential converts, but patience was sorely tried on Lena. The preachers' frustration was held in check to simmer under Sunday smiles.

Lena attended each church erratically. Her absence and presence was duly noted on the rolls kept by each congregation, while she divided up the Sundays equally for each church. One by one, the pastors approached Lena to ask the same question, "Sister Lena, do you know what you are doing? All these churches you been agoing to . . . they ain't the same."

Lena pursed her lips. The wrinkles in her face settled into a hint of a smile. She nodded her scarfed head, "I'm gonna church. Be with Jesus."

"But Sister Lena," the pastors went on to say, "these churches don't all believe the same way."

Lena's sunken eyes widened. "Oh?" she asked with a naive smile.

Each pastor answered, "No. You see, Sister Lena, we have different rules we go by. We believe that God wants us to live in a certain way and it's very different from the way those people in other churches live. Otherwise, we'd all be alike. Wouldn't make much difference what church we went to."

Lena sat for a while and looked into her grandchild's eyes. Then she looked at the church pastor she spoke to and said, "Ever since I a little girl, some peoples, they tole me that. But it don't matter, it's alla same."

The preachers in a state of exasperation would say, "No, it's not the same, Sister Lena. You don't understand."

141

Lena would then purse her lips and nod her head again. "It's alla same. Yes, it is. Alla same. You don't understand."

Often Lena's response would end the conversation there. But one time a boyish preacher visited Lena's home to "try to talk some sense into her dense old head" as he himself said. He wore a black suit and tie, even though the sun was unbearable that day.

"Save your soul, Sister Lena," he said outside her house. "You getting old. Someday soon now, you going to die."

Lena's face settled into a playful smile again. She looked off into the hills. She answered, "Face death ever day I live. Ever thing dies. It does. Shouldn't come as no surprise." As she talked, a mosquito landed on her wrist. She slapped it. She went on, "It happens like that. One day, you walking round and round. Next day you dead like this one here. Life's gone out. Thems the way things are. Don't worry bout that. Boy, you sceered to die?"

The preacher's pink face became red. Lena couldn't tell if he was angry or not. "No, I'm not scared to die!" he said. "I'm worried about you. Me, I'm saved. You . . . You going to burn in Hell unless you're saved. And then the Devil will rejoice. He's won!" He wiped his red face with a damp, limp handkerchief.

Lena's grandchild had been playing in the distance. She had been crawling around in the dirt for some time. She came running to Lena then. Her face dripped with sweat. She said, "Grandma, looky here." She held her hand up to Lena.

Lena answered her, "Not now, baby. This man here, he's been trying to say something." The grandchild sat on the bench beside the preacher, her fingers clutched together.

The preacher continued louder than before, "As I was saying, Sister Lena, Hell is hot. You'll burn for eternity. Do you know how long that is?"

Lena wiped the child's face with the printed skirt of her faded dress. "It's lotta lifetimes. Too many to count. Too long to remember," she said. Her smile was gone and her voice was wistful. Thoughtfully, she looked at her gray house that once was white, then back to her grandchild again.

The preacher feared he'd lost her attention. He added quickly, "Don't give the Devil that chance to rejoice, Sister! He's evil! And Hell is hot!" He took off his suit jacket and threw it beside him as if to emphasize what he said.

Lena studied the tall, lanky white preacher with the sweat rolling down his neck. She was definitely interested in what he said, he could tell. His chest puffed out a bit to think he'd done it, scared some sense into her. Then she said, "Oklahoma must be like Hell a lot. It's sure hot!" The preacher was momentarily speechless. Lena continued, "The Debil? Well, you right bout him, preacher. I heered stories bout him. Seen him once too. Know what he looks like."

The preacher deflated like a punctured balloon. "Sister Lena," he enunciated each syllable angrily, "you don't know what the Devil looks like! What are you talking about?"

Lena rose from the upside-down can she sat on and walked to the preacher. Face to face with her, he saw the wrinkles in her face shift around as she bent to him and said, "Lissen here, I know." She whispered to the excited man, "He looks like you. Yes, he does. The Debil does. Looks jest like you."

His face went through several contortions before he was able to speak coherently. Lena's grandchild watched him go through the range of emotions. He blurted out several words. Lena knew two languages and couldn't make out what he said in either one of them. She wondered if he knew himself what he said. When he had calmed down somewhat, he told Lena, "Sister Lena, you're trying my patience."

Lena herself was patient with him as he recovered control. Eventually he wore a tight strained smile and managed to ask, "Why do you come to church anyway, Sister Lena? Do you believe in God?"

Lena answered without hesitation, "Because alla these peoples, they ask me to come. Sides, I like it. Jesus I like. The songs too."

The preacher shook his head and seemed to understand. He asked, "What do you know about God or Jesus?"

"Not too much. Jest what I heered over yonder in church," she admitted cheerfully.

He became more confident then and boldly said, "I hear you people don't have religion. Don't believe in God or Jesus."

For the first time in their conversation, Lena's mouth clamped shut. Her lips pursed tightly. She looked at him with open distrust and sat down again on the makeshift chair. She looked at the girl and said, "I'll tell you what I can. We don't got Jesus. We got something else. It's ever thing. Hard to sit and talk bout it. Can't say it in so many words. So we sing, we dance. What we have is a mystery. Don't got answers for it, and don't understand it. But its all right. Jest live right in it. Side by side."

"You talking superstition now Sister Lena," the preacher said. "Ain't nothing to it. That's whats wrong with you people. Better put that stuff behind you. For the sake of your grandchild there, if nothing else." He pointed at the little girl who watched his every move.

Lena answered him, "Thank you, preacher, but we came this far. Us peoples. Been looking out for ourselves. Came this far since the beginning. This girl's gonna know jest how things are."

When the preacher stood to leave, Lena's face was bright as she promised, "We see you at church come Sunday, preacher." He scowled while Lena giggled and the child waved.

When the preacher's car rolled between the hills, Lena turned to her grandchild and asked, "Now what is it?"

The girl held up her hand and showed Lena three little eggs. "Thems snake eggs, baby," Lena said. "Take them back and put them where they was."

That evening when the day's work was done, Lena and the grandchild sat outside in the breeze. Lena asked, "Baby, you put them snake eggs back like I tole you?" The grandchild nodded. Darkness descended upon them while Lena talked. "They's lotsa snakes hereabouts, baby." Her voice threw the words through the hills. "Got to watch. Some of these snakes, they's harmless. And some's poison. Got to know which is which. Those green and black snakes, they nothing. They mind their own business. Let them pass. Leave all of them alone. My father, he tole me, daughter—you can't always see them snakes but you gonna know when you git bit."

For nights after, Lena's words bounced back to the child's ears until she knew them as well as she knew each line in her grandmother's face and hands. But for then, she sat and remembered all the snakes she'd met in the hills and creeks. She knew that even as she sat with Lena there, snakes hung in the trees around them, hissing with long and delicate tongues as they did when she climbed the trees to examine them. That very morning when she collected eggs from the chicken coop, her chubby fingers groped a blacksnake instead of eggs. It had stolen them. The eggshells were completely intact, with tiny holes drilled into them, where the snake sucked the eggs out.

Lena was saying, "Got to watch your step. Look round and lissen!" The child nodded her head in the darkness, her face wore a serious expression.

The star patterns slowly slid across the sky. The grandchild lifted her finger and began to count the stars. Then she remembered the preacher and she turned to Lena. She asked Lena, "That whiteman was sure mad at us today, huh?"

Lena's silhouette nodded under the stars.

"Why, Grandma? How come he acted mean with us?" the girl wanted to know.

Lena began to unravel the girl's braids. "Not his fault, baby," she said. "He's jest young. And he thinks he knows ever thing."

"You shoulda tole him bout things, Grandma," the grandchild said as she hugged the old lady protectively.

Lena squeezed the chubby arms clinging around her and said, "Wouldn't do no good, baby. He don't lissen. Don't hear the wind and the rain, the trees, and the grass. Don't hear it, the voice inside the mystery." Lena pulled the pins out of her white hair and it fell free over her shoulders.

She stood and stretched. The girl grabbed Lena's skirts and followed to the heavy metal bed with broken springs where they slept in good weather. Lena opened the quilts. She and her grandchild lay down to rest.

"They purty, huh, Grandma?" the young one asked and pointed to the twinkling stars.

"Stars is pretty, all right," Lena agreed.

"Hey Grandma," the child lay on her belly and looked at Lena. "Is ever thing purty like stars?"

Lena's eyes glittered much like the stars above her. She answered, "Baby, it depends on how you look at it. They's somethings in the world whats not too pretty. They's people, mostly."

The child put a chubby hand on Lena's face as she told her grandmother, "You purty, Grandma. Got eyes like stars."

Lena laughed and said, "We can't see ever thing what's in the world, baby. They's lotsa things in the world sides jest what we see."

The child was immediately curious. She moved closer to her grandmother. Lena straightened the blankets saying, "We not the only ones what lives. Us peoples knows. Some others maybe think they's the only ones what live. And too, things ain't always what they look like. We walk round and round—moving through life. Life so big. It mysterious and it all round us, ever where. Lotsa times though, us peoples can't see whats round us. It gonna be there though, sure enough."

Lena's and the grandchild's forms fused with darkness. Both were motionless while Lena spoke, "Out there—they's a lot what lives and moves. Us peoples knows it because it touches us. Then us peoples seem like little things next to it. It big and mysterious. Yes, lotsa times us peoples feel it, if we want to or not. It jest touches us and us peoples thinks we's part of it."

Lena tapped the child lightly on a wrist and the child felt it with her entire body. "That's how it is," Lena said to her. "Jest like that. That's how come we knows they's other things in the world sides only what we see. Us peoples been thinking this since the first day. Don't hardly talk bout it much tween ourselves. Can't say much bout something what's plain as day. But you jest a baby, so I tole you. Gonna help you out a little, so you can go a long ways."

The little girl's eyes darted about in the darkness, exploring it for what she did not see in it. A bright star fell on her and Lena. A path of streaking light sprinkled the house. The child's thoughts went to the preacher again. Then the girl bit her tongue but could not stop a question. "What does the Devil look like, Grandma?"

Lena rolled to her side and looked her grandchild in the face. She told the girl, "Well, some says he's red and has horns and a long tail. But they's others who says he's handsome and can make hisself look like anything he wants to look like."

"Is the Devil a man?" the grandchild asked.

Lena watched airplane lights flicker in the sky. It was a while before she replied. "I don't know, baby. Maybe. Some Indian peoples though says the Debil is a whiteman." Lena coughed as she spoke. The words came spitting out. The girl thought that Lena smiled when she said that, but could not know for sure in the dark. Everything was quiet, except for the plane that plowed through the stars. Just when the girl thought Lena was asleep, Lena said, "Got to watch for him, baby. Look and lissen, like you do round snakes. Jest pick your steps round him."

"Who you talking bout, Grandma?" the girl asked. "The Devil?"

Lena did laugh then in a soft voice. She promised, "Baby, the time's a coming.

You gonna see. I gonna be there though. See you through it. But baby, after that, you on your own." Lena squeezed the girl's plump hand and held onto it until both slept soundly. Around them, the wind gently blew and the trees and the grass danced in the darkness.

Three years had passed, Lena's grandchild was eight. She was thinner, but her eyes had grown to twice their size. Lena and the girl sat on their broken bed and surveyed the camp in the evening.

About three hundred canvas tents were scattered along the creek banks. A few cars, mostly 1950 models, were parked beside the tents. Wagons were more numerous. Horses grazed in the pasture beyond the narrow creek that wound about the camp on three sides. Pecan and cottonwood trees shaded the tents with filtered sunlight during the hottest part of the day. That day it had reached 105 in the shade. In the evening it cooled though and must have been in the lower 90s then. Lena fanned herself with one of the girl's comic books.

They had eaten and a small cooking fire sent tendrils of smoke up into the trees. It hung there without any breeze to dissipate it. Around them, other small cooking fires burned and the sound of people's voices drifted back and forth across the creek. Something dropped out of the tree limbs over them and landed at Lena's and the girl's feet. It was a twig. The girl looked up toward the tree but could not see anything in the shadows.

"It's a tree snake," Lena told her. "Harmless. After a big old nest up yonder. Been up there for days, since we got here."

"How do you know, Grandma?" the girl asked Lena.

Lena answered, "I seen him. Spotted him as soon as we got here. Ain't gonna bother us none."

Bells began to jingle in the tents near them and far away. Drumbeats came down the creek banks to them. Lena and the girl could see the men who would dance shake their bright feathered bustles and hang them on the tents and wagons. The bustles looked like shields from a distance.

Lena went into the tent and called her grandchild. Lena helped the girl put on a black skirt with rows of satin and silk ribbons at the hem and down the front of the skirt. The ribbons were brilliant hues of color. Over the skirt, Lena pulled a dark pink satin shirt over the girl's head. Ribbons ran across the shoulders in the front and back of the blouse. Above these ribbons were metal ornaments about the size of quarters scattered randomly across the top of the blouse. Lena tied several bright scarves at the girl's neck and hung several strands of black glass beads over the scarves. The beads were heavy and swung down below the girl's waist. Next Lena stuck some beads into the girl's braids. The girl was ready when she slipped on a pair of black moccasins. As the two left the tent, Lena handed the girl a dark pink shawl with long fringes for use when the girl danced.

In the next tent an old man sang to himself. Drumbeats floated down the creek and became muted in the trees as Lena and the girl walked through the encampment on their way to the evening's dance. At two tents they stopped to visit relatives. By the time they arrived, activities were underway.

Lena had brought her own metal folding chair from their tent. She unfolded it and put it behind the white painted benches the dancers used. Then Lena settled down to visit with a woman next to her. Half a dozen men dancers sat in front of Lena on the white benches. The girl took a place on the bench beside the men dancers. She had decided on arrival that something was peculiar about the evening, but was unable then to say exactly what it was. Her large eyes went around the dance arena, over the dancers and other tribal people there.

The sun hid itself behind the hill where the agency building was constructed. A string of electric light bulbs that circled the dance arena suddenly lit. An announcer at the speaker's stand welcomed the crowd. His voice went out over the public address system, "Aho! We greet all our relatives and guests tonight. Welcome to the first night of our annual gathering." The girl knew that his speech would be long. She became restless. Lena gave her some coins for a soft drink. She disappeared into the standing crowd behind the rows of folding chairs that people had brought and set up. The girl took her time getting her refreshment and returning. She could hear each speaker through the microphone and when the drum began to pound and the songs began, she started back. She leaned on Lena's arm and tried to figure out what was so different about the night.

A few dancers were dancing in a round dance line. They moved counter-clockwise around the arena, in a shuffling step. Fringes swayed brilliantly under the string of light bulbs. Men in furry hats or feathered head-dresses moved with more energy than did the women. The line bobbed up and down as the dancers moved around the arena. The girl laid the pink shawl over her arm and joined the dancers at the end of the line. She looked much like the other dancers. As the girl danced, she studied the faces of the observers. The girl saw that Lena watched her approvingly and noticed too that Lena watched someone else. Lena's face fell briefly into a frown, her eyes narrowed and her lips pursed. Then she looked at the girl and smiled calmly across the dance arena.

After that dance ended, the girl returned to her seat. Lena was bent toward her neighbor, the woman was whispering something into Lena's ear. The girl then realized there was no laughter, or joking, or teasing conversation that usually accompanied these gatherings. That was what was different! Everyone spoke in whispers. The girl's eyes moved from Lena to others who all were whispering to each other around the arena.

Another dance began. The crowd around the girl was murmuring among themselves and pointed to someone in the newly formed line of dancers. The girl wanted to know who it was. The beginning of the dance line was approaching. The girl quickly counted nearly forty dancers. They passed in front of her in a snake-like line. The girl studied the people sitting around her again. No one sang along with the singers as was common, or tapped their fingers, or feet, to the drum. The people were rigid in their seats and leaned toward the dancers. The line danced by, in front of her. The girl watched the last dancer pass. Then a buzz of whispers filled the air.

"Grandma," she tugged at Lena's taffeta sleeve, "What's going on?" she asked. The girl's voice was loud over the whispers. She sat on the bench and leaned back to Lena. Lena's eyes sparkled like the black glass beads the girl wore. Lena put a finger over her own lips and motioned the girl to be silent and watch. The girl obeyed and sat quietly through the dance, watching the strange behavior around her.

Another song started. The head dancers were the first to rise. The man moved out first. The feathers on his head and arms began to shake and swirl. The woman was dressed in pale yellows. Her dance was a startling contrast to the man's. She was demure, dignified, and restrained in her steps. Her feet were soft and made no sound or impression on the ground. She held her head high and straight. In her right hand, she carried a large eagle wing fan. Other dancers rose to join the head dancers after a few seconds.

The girl searched the group of dancers for her favorite clown. He was a humorous old man who pranced and paraded before the ladies when he danced. He was so vain. He always donned mixed-up dancing clothes that were forbidden for other dancers but were his trademark. All the undesirable qualities in a dancer is what he represented. He brought the tribal people much joy with his foolish dancing ways. Yes, the clown was there sitting on a bench, but he had not moved the whole evening. The girl thought that very strange!

Another dance started. It was a two-step, adapted from the white community. The head dancers lead the column of dancers again. This time though, several dancers seemed undecided as to whether or not they would dance. A few did begin to dance but then abruptly returned to the benches and sat stiffly down. About a dozen couples continued to dance. Most of them wore confused expressions on their faces.

The people sitting with Lena watched someone in the file of dancers. Their whispers were loud and the girl tried to make out what they said. They spoke in Indian and it was all muffled. Lena frowned and pursed her lips. A tense feeling was in the air. The people seemed to have gone from apprehension to anger and indignation.

The girl knew most of the dancers either through kinship or by their dancing reputation. The first eight couples were all adults. The young people were next. Each lady who danced wore a shawl over her street clothes or dance dress, but a few of the men danced in street wear and cowboy boots.

The girl squinted her eyes to block out the glare of the light bulbs. She saw that not all the men dancers were Indian. Three were not. The girl was related to most of the Indian men. One of the whitemen was married into the tribe, so he was considered one of them.

Suddenly, Lena grabbed the girl's arm and pulled the girl onto her lap. The girl was too old for this and Lena was so small, Lena hadn't held her this way for a long time. The girl soon saw why this was done.

An old lady, older than Lena, made her way towards them from the crowd behind. The old lady stopped beside the girl and Lena. The old lady's eyes were cloudy as she laid them on the tribal people around her. She looked at Lena and nodded to her. Lena returned the gesture. The old lady looked at the girl. "Hi, Grandma," the girl said without hesitation, as she did to all the old women. The old lady paid the girl no attention. The girl thought the old lady's cloudy eyes burned like embers for an instant. Then the old lady turned away from the girl and watched the dancers. The old lady's presence was observed carefully by other tribal members.

The old lady watched one of the whitemen. He was unfamiliar to the girl. He danced with one of the tribe's young women. The woman was of French and Indian ancestry. She had inherited her great-grandfather's French name and his fair complexion. She wore a red dance dress and her partner was in a gray cowboy suit with a white cowboy hat. Lena's grandchild thought this whiteman quite handsome.

The old lady at the girl's side muttered something to herself. She turned to Lena and looked down at her. She said only one word to Lena. The girl had never heard it before. The old lady said it softly; it was almost a whisper. Her body seemed to deflate and shrink with the pronouncement of the word. The old lady's cloudy eyes sternly looked at the dancing cowboy once more. The dance had ended. The cloudy eyes followed as he escorted the young woman to a chair across the arena. Everyone watched him.

The girl in Lena's arms watched the old lady as she turned back into the crowd without saying another word and disappeared into the darkness that hovered over the electric light bulbs and all around.

BOOM! BOOM! The drum made muffled tones and a high-pitched man's voice began to sing. Other singers, male and female, soon joined in, continuing the evening dance. But there was commotion in the speaker's stand.

Lena's gaze had never left the whiteman on the far side of the arena. Lena pointed to him and held her finger in front of the girl's eyes, so the child could see him. He was in the company of another young woman. They casually strolled to the dance area. He was much taller than she as he danced at her side, clumsy and a bit out of step with the other men. His partner, on the other hand, was graceful and small. Members of the tribe were rising from their seats to stand and watch this couple. Children stood on tiptoe and pushed people away and clothing which blocked their view.

As the whiteman and his young woman danced in front of Lena and the girl, the people actually pointed at him openly. Whispers were louder than before. The people were definitely angry. Suddenly, the drum stopped, in the middle of a song . . . ! The few dancers quickly dispersed.

The whiteman led the young woman to her chair. The girl, still in Lena's arms, saw the young woman's mother meet her daughter and the whiteman halfway there. The mother pulled on the daughter's arm, and away from the man. The young woman's face wore surprise and embarrassment at her mother's behavior, but the daughter surrendered and left with her mother. The whiteman simply moved on, acting as if he was totally unaware of the commotion that he caused. He stopped in front of two more young women and by their smiles, even Lena's grandchild knew he would stay there for a while.

Several minutes passed. The singers had abandoned the drum. Static came over the public address system. Then a voice called through the microphone, "My relatives, we are going to cancel the rest of the evening's activities. Gather your families and return to your tents. Remain there for the rest of the night." The words hung in the air with the camp smoke and darkness. The announcement was repeated twice, once in English, and once in the tribal tongue. People began to move toward their tents. Lena folded her chair as she talked to others in barely audible tones.

The girl saw that a crowd had collected around the whiteman in the gray suit; it was made up mostly of admiring young women. The old lady who appeared out of the darkness earlier was then approaching this group. The old lady momentarily stood beneath a wavering yellow light bulb that cast an unearthly glow on her. She put a withered hand on one of the women who stood on the outskirts of the group. The old lady said something to the young woman. The young woman's smooth face became contorted, she turned and fled.

A few men were helping the people leave. The people at the dance arena had thinned by half, but the remainder were moving out slowly. The microphone screeched and came alive. A breathless male voice said something in Indian, then in English. It said, "My relatives, the Devil is among us tonight. Take your families to your tents! Stay there!" The people began to scurry.

The whiteman with his crowd of women admirers paid no attention to the loudspeaker. He walked towards Lena and her grandchild. The girl darted toward him before Lena knew it. Only four or five feet away from him, the girl's curiosity had peaked. She rushed in to have a look at him. The top of his white felt hat was visible. She squeezed through the ladies surrounding him. His clothing was within reach. She could not see his face. The girl's hand went out to touch him. Just as her fingers opened, the girl was yanked away from him by the neck of her blouse.

Lena swatted the girl twice and led her to their tent. All the way to the tent, Lena did not release the hold on the girl's blouse. The girl thought that she would choke.

Lena pulled the girl into their tent and lit the coal-oil lamp. She dumped the girl into bed, dance clothes and all. Then Lena blew out the lamp and sat a long time on the broken bed, beside the girl.

The girl lay there and listened to the camp. It made no sound. Its presence under the trees might never be known, she thought. There were no camp lights, no voices, no movement of any kind. The electric light bulbs over the dance arena had been unplugged and camp fires had died. The only sound of life the girl heard was Lena's breathing and her own heart beating in the corner of their tent. The girl could not resist opening the tent flap Lena had closed. She looked outside at the dark, silent camp.

"What do you see?" Lena whispered into the girl's ear.

The girl answered, "Nothing, Grandma."

Lena's face turned toward the girl. Lena's eyes blinked and shone in the dark. She whispered, "Look again."

Lena woke the girl just after sunrise. "Gonna pull the tent down and go on home, baby," she said. The girl was momentarily disappointed because she always liked these gatherings. Still dressed in last night's rumpled clothing, the girl went outside and looked around. The tent that had been next to them was already gone. Only a clear square piece of ground hinted that anything had been there. Other tents were being dismantled.

The girl went back inside the tent to change. She closed the tent flaps for privacy. Someone approached the side of the tent. A female voice said, "Sister Lena, will you have a way to get home, you and the girl?"

Lena answered, "Sent word this morning. We be gone by midday. Someone will come." Lena was cooking for the girl.

The voice said again, "Sister Lena, they found another one. That's three now." As the girl changed her clothing, she listened.

Lena sat down on the bench beside the table. The girl knew because the bench always squeaked under the slightest weight. Lena answered, "Don't come as no surprise. Who are they?"

The other voice said, "I don't know. They all danced with him, though. One simply did not wake this morning. One passed in the night. This one they are talking about now, I really don't know the details. Do the details matter?"

The girl imagined that Lena was shaking her head, no.

The voice went on, "Well, Sister Lena, we're ready to leave, so I have to go now. I suppose you will want to help put these girls away?"

With her braids undone and her hair hanging loose, the girl came out of the tent. Lena was nodding to the caller.

151

"Well, baby, gonna eat now. Got lots to do. Be evening before we sit down again," Lena said.

The girl sat down at the table and spooned cooked cereal into her mouth. The tree leaves above the girl and Lena rustled. The girl looked up. A large black snake was wound around the overhanging limb. The girl made a face at it. She stuck out her tongue at it like the snakes often did to her. She laid down her spoon, looked at Lena and asked, "How did you know, Grandma?"

Lena answered, "It's happened before. Seen some things before. Us peoples knows lotsa things. Jest keeps it to ourselves. Now, come on, eat. Be too hot to move soon."

"Like Hell?" the girl asked Lena.

Lena swallowed her cereal and said, "Looks to me like you learning, baby."

I'm Making You Up

Grandma we all need   partially deaf & busy with weaving   listens
    through a thick blanket of years & sore feet
        nods
I cry about everything they did to me   how horrible   & can't stand another
while brown wrinkled you smile at me like sun coming up
    I stand next to you, pass wool absently   you lay aside the wrong colors
        without comment
I'm simply
Grandchild
  babbling   your sympathy warm & comforting as dust
    I sit in your lap   your loom pushed aside
        you feed me fry bread with too much maple syrup
      I pull your braids   you cradle me deeper in   your legs folded to make
        a basket for me
Grandma who died long before I was born
    Come Back
        Come Back

Elaine Hall

Spider, World-Spinner

Spider, world-spinner
    a baby in this life
like you, I feel just-hatched
Scurrying out of the way of the
      bath water, you find refuge in
      a crack of the plaster
(Some of the People found refuge
in cliff dwellings cut out of red stone)

Spider, world-spinner
I think of how the sound of water
      teaches us
A music that sings about
      fear, betrayal,
      grocery money to be counted out
      against a hungry day.
My ancestors
      forced to leave their home
      days of hunger made madder
      by the hands of enemies
      snatching food from the mouths
      of nursing mothers

Spider, world-spinner
    my memories unroll
    like a line of spit
You and I have a memory older still

A memory of the time
    you swallowed a previous world
Swallowed and started
    over again

Elaine Hall

Spider Dream

I woke this morning and sunlight
    scalded my face
I went into the kitchen to make tea
    saw a spider drinking from the tap
(I say sunlight scalded my face, but
    my window faces west)

The spider's egg-sac was full
I went to bed and slept awhile
My left leg hurt in my sleep and
    when I woke again, I saw
    an open sore running the length
    of an old scar
(I had injured that leg on a tin can
    when I was five)

In this open scar gleamed the eggs
    Mother-Spider had buried in me
Spiders, new life, hatching
    running out in all directions
To find water
    or forgiveness
    or
    a way to be.

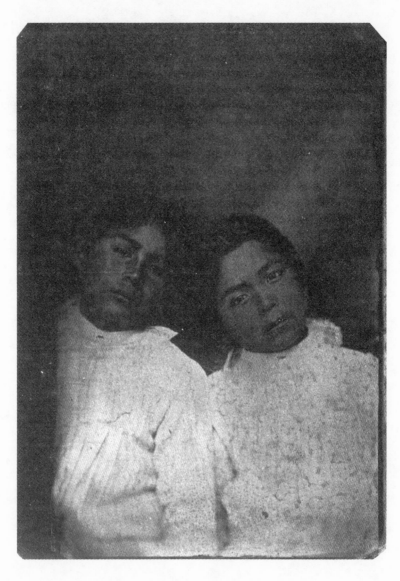

Tintype from the collection of Joy Harjo

Anita Endrezze-Danielson

October Morning Walk

for Aaron, age 2

On the pond, frost floats like rice paper,
cattails exclaiming the absence of mallards.
Between frost and water, drowned wasps
promise the water its one dream: to fly.
Algae begins its elegy, lamenting summer.
Aaron, circling the pond, kicks the thistles
whose ragged heads are in a final drowse.
Over us, the last sharp-shinned hawk
robs the air of its patented horizon.
In this cold, I hunger for a field of suns
while my son day-dreams about a moon
as white as a feather and an owl
whose eyes are icy moons in an empty sky.
Aaron is Autumn's child. I follow him
into the dark-tufted meadow where frost's
fragile language sparkles on his tongue.

Joy Harjo

From the Salt Lake City Airport – 82

This place is white
like salt. An ocean began
and nearly ended.
Ghost moons skim
along the gut depths
make their way
into the airport, watching
the travelers
for news of home, for some change
that might have taken place
without them, then slip back
to wait.

The Wasatch Mountains plead
to be remembered.
in the East.
They watched wagon trails
wear down men, allowed them
to cross their bellies
thinking these white-skins
could learn to love this land
as much as them, and the darker ones
already here.
Allowed the god they loved
to enter with them,
a god who grew bitter and hard
and looked only West.

And these people learned
how to eat off the salty plain,
they built a city
of separation.
Grew children
and named them names of men,
another language
not the land.

And they are white.

It is a crazy, dangerous joke
to forget the red hills
that border your city
with passion.
They are mirrors
that make you hate yourself
for what you didn't
want to remember.
Salt Lake City,
you grow hot and ashamed
when you look East,
and feel uncomfortable
with the power of the womb,
and place the blame
on the devil
and your wives.

You are hiding much more
than just names in the vault
of your church.

I see your women caught behind windows
in their homes, behind rows and rows
of bleached and frightened children.
They speak men's words, not their own
except those languages they've
learned to speak in secret
and in dreams, if they've
not forgotten.

I see tribes
gathering themselves together
not for war, but for recognition.
They didn't disappear
when your god's name was spoken.
Not all were swallowed by
a hopeless misery.

There is still the sun
rising over the Wasatch
to the East, blanketing them
sweetening them.

The earth does break open and spill
by the quakings of the heart
by forces other than man.
The lake of salt that floats
West of here feeds you.
She is the womb of your discomfort,
your mother, a ghost
you could easily disrupt.

Let it break open, Salt Lake City.
Listen to what forms the earth
what breathes, even beneath your
shiny new airport, where I watch your
blonde and silent women.

Let your memory break open.

When we die
all our bodies darken
into rich, scarlet
woman earth.

When we die
our bodies turn to salt
but our spirits are shimmering
colored stars
and we are food.

Mary Moran

Barbara

Barbara shed her clothes and stuffed them
into the nearly-full laundry bag.
Her discards were swallowed-up whole.
The belly of the bag bulged and rested
on the cool tile floor in contented silence
until tomorrow's trip to the laundromat
where the cockroaches lived in the seams
of the washing machines.

The shower water started lukewarm.
She turned the knob around to HOT.
What does not wash away will be steamed out.
She scrubs and scrubs her skin to rid it
of polyester, plastic, and yellow paint.

At the welfare office she had sat for four hours
on the same green plastic chair waiting for her name
to be called. (If she got up she would have lost
her seat and had to join the group of standing waiters.)
She moved within the chair, to shift her wait,
to exhaust all the possibilities for comfort.

The yellow paint on the walls in the waiting room
had a semi-gloss finish that reflected the needy.
Loosely grouped people stood against the walls
smoking cigarettes and reading sections of the day's paper.
Asian, Latino, Black, and Anglo tongues
mixed, separated, mixed back together again,
sounding just one-level-tone below
that of the social worker's name-calling.
A baby cried; another answered.
Three people huddled together in the back
laughed at a joke they were sharing.

Twice the phone rang.
Twice a young Black man answered it
and called out a name.
Twice no one claimed that name.
Half the waiting people laughed while others simply smiled.
And some people just sat the whole time staring at the floor
until they were called by their case workers.

Her eyes wandered through the crowd
recognizing layers of Goodwill, Salvation
Army, and St. Vincent de Paul.
She saw the new clothes. Polyester dresses,
shirts and pants from K-Mart and Woolworths.
Several men were wearing shoes that didn't quite fit.
Fifty-cent to one dollar plastic shopping bags
leaned against some older women's legs.
Barbara doesn't wear polyester anymore.
The fabric doesn't breathe.
It had made her sweat and smell bad.
Her skin suffocated and rashes emerged in protest.
In this place her body remembers polyester.
It was the material of her maid
and waitress uniforms, the fabric
of the jobs she couldn't hold onto.
She had wanted to leave, but stayed instead
and waited for her name to be called.

Carol Lee Sanchez

Sex, Class and Race Intersections
Visions of Women of Color

"As I understand it," said the American Indian [to one of the Puritan Fathers], "you propose to civilize me."
"Exactly."
"You want to get me out of the habit of idleness and teach me to work."
"That is the idea."
"And then lead me to simplify my methods and invent things to make my work lighter."
"Yes."
"And after that I'll become ambitious to get rich so that I won't have to work at all."
"Naturally."
"Well what's the use of taking such a roundabout way of getting just where I started from? I don't have to work now."

(American Jokelore)

To identify Indian is to identify with an invisible or vanished people; it is to identify with a set of basic assumptions and beliefs held by *all* who are not Indian about the indigenous peoples of the Americas. Even among the Spanish-speaking Mestizos or mezclados, there is a strong preference to "disappear" their Indian blood, to disassociate from their Indian beginnings. To be Indian is to be considered "colorful," spiritual, connected to the earth, simplistic, and disappointing if not dressed in buckskin and feathers; shocking if a city-dweller and even more shocking if an educator or other type of professional. That's the positive side.

On the negative side, to be Indian is to be thought of as primitive, alcoholic, ignorant (as in "Dumb Indian"), better off dead (as in "the only good Indian is a dead Indian" or "I didn't know there was any of you folks still left"), unskilled, non-competitive, immoral, pagan or heathen, untrustworthy (as in "Indian-giver") and frightening. To be Indian is to be the primary model that is used to promote racism in this country.

How can that happen, you ask? Bad press. One hundred and fifty years of the most consistently vicious press imaginable. Newspapers, dime novels, textbooks and fifty years of visual media have portrayed and continue to portray Indians as savage, blood-thirsty, immoral, inhuman people. When there's a touch of social consciousness attached, you will find the once "blood-thirsty," "white-killer savage" portrayed as a pitiful drunk, a loser, an outcast or a mix-blood not welcomed by, or

163

trusted by, either race. For fifty years, children in this country have been raised to kill Indians mentally, subconsciously through the visual media, until it is an automatic reflex. That shocks you? Then I have made my point.

Let me quote from Helen Hunt Jackson's book, *A Century of Dishonor*, from the introduction written by Bishop H. B. Whipple of Minnesota, who charged that:

> the American people have accepted as truth the teachings that the Indians were a degraded, brutal race of savages, who it was the will of God should perish at the approach of civilization. If they do not say with our Puritan fathers that these are the Hittites who are to be driven out before the saints of the Lord, they do accept the teaching that manifest destiny will drive the Indians from the earth. The inexorable has no tears or pity at the cries of anguish of the doomed race.

This race still struggles to stay alive. Tribe by Tribe, pockets of Indian people here and there. One million two hundred thousand people who identify as Indians—raised and socialized as Indian—as of the 1980 census, yet Cowboys and Indians is still played every day by children all over America of every creed, color, and nationality. Well—it's harmless isn't it? Just kids playing kill Indians. It's all history. But it's still happening every day, and costumes are sold and the cheap western is still rolling out of Hollywood, the old shoot-'em-up westerns playing on afternoon kid shows, late night T.V. Would you allow your children to play Nazis and Jews? Blacks and KKKs? Complete with costume? Yes! It is a horrifying thought, but in thinking about it you can see how easy it is to dismiss an entire race of people as barbaric and savage, and how almost impossible it is, after this has been inculcated in you, to relate to an Indian or a group of Indians today. For example, how many famous Indians do you know offhand? Certainly the great warrior chiefs come to mind first, and of course the three most famous Indian "Princesses"—Pocahantas, Sacajawea and La Malinche. Did you get past ten? Can you name at least five Indian women you know personally or have heard about? That's just counting on one hand, folks.

As Indians, we have endured. We are still here. We have survived everything that European "civilization" has imposed on us. There are approximately 130 different Indian languages still spoken in North America of the some 300 spoken at contact; 180 different Tribes incorporated and recognized by the Federal Government of the approximately 280 that once existed, with an additional 15 to 25 unrecognized Tribes that are lumped together on a reservation with other Tribes. We still have Women's Societies and there are at least 30 active women-centered Mother-Rite Cultures existing and practicing their everyday life in that manner, on this continent.

We have been displaced, relocated, removed, terminated, educated, acculturated and in our hearts and minds we will always "go back to the blanket" as long as we are still connected to our families, our Tribes and our land.

164

The Indian Way is a different way. It is a respectful way. The basic teachings in every Tribe that exists today as a Tribe in the western hemisphere are based on respect for all the things our Mother gave us. If we neglect her or anger her, she will make our lives very difficult and we always know that we have a hardship on ourselves and on our children. We are raised to be cautious and concerned for the *future* of our people, and that is how we raise our children—because *they* are *our* future. Your "civilization" has made all of us very sick and has made our mother earth sick and out of balance. Your kind of thinking and education has brought the whole world to the brink of total disaster, whereas the thinking and education among my people forbids the practice of almost everything Euro-Americans, in particular, value.

Those of you who are socialists and marxists have an ideology, but where in this country do you live communally on a common land base from generation to generation? Indians, who have a way of life instead of an ideology, do live on communal lands and don't accumulate anything—for the sake of accumulation.

Radicals look at reservation Indians and get very upset about their poverty conditions. But poverty to us is not the same thing as poverty is to you. Our poverty is that we can't be who we are. We can't hunt or fish or grow our food because our basic resources and the right to use them in traditional ways are denied us. In order to live well, we must be able to provide for ourselves in such a way that we can continue living as we always have. We still don't believe in being slaves to the "domineering" culture systems. Consequently, we are accused of many things based on those standards and values that make no sense to us.

You want us to act like you, to be like you so that we will be more acceptable, more likeable. You should try to be more like us regarding communal co-existence; respect and care for all living things and for the earth, the waters, and the atmosphere; respect for human dignity and the right to be who they are.

During the 1930s, '40s and '50s, relocation programs caused many Indians to become lost in the big cities of the United States and there were many casualties from alcoholism, vagrancy and petty crime. Most Indians were/are jailed for assault and battery in barroom brawls because the spiritual and psychological violation of Indian people trying to live in the dominant [domineering] culture generally forces us to numb ourselves as frequently as possible. That is difficult, if not impossible, for you to understand. White science studies dead things and creates poisonous substances to kill and maim the creatures as well as the humans. You call that progress. Indians call it insanity. Our science studies living things; how they interact and how they maintain a balanced existence. Your science disregards—even denies—the spirit world: ours believes in it and remains connected to it. We fast, pray to our ancestors, call on them when we dance and it rains—at Laguna, at Acoma, at Hopi—still, today. We fight among ourselves, we have border disputes, we struggle to exist in a modern context with our lands full of timber, uranium, coal, oil, gasoline, precious metals and semi-precious stones; full—because we are taught to take only what we need and not because we are too ignorant to know what to do with all these resources. We are caught in the bind between private corporations and the government—"our guardian"—because they/you want all those resources. "Indians certainly don't need them"—and your people will do *anything* to get their hands on our mineral-rich lands. They will legislate, stir up internal conflicts, cause inter-Tribal conflicts, dangle huge amounts of monies as compensation for perpetual contracts and promise lifetime economic security. If we object, or sue to protect our lands, these suits will be held in litigation for fifteen to twenty years with "white" interests benefiting in the interim. Some of us give up and sell out, but there are many of us learning to hold out and many many more of us going back to the old ways of thinking, because we see that our ancestors were right and that the old ways were better ways. So, more Indians are going "back to the blanket," back to "Indian time," with less stress, fewer dominant (domineering) culture activities and occupations. Modern Indians are recreating Indian ways once again. All this leads to my vision as an Indian woman. It is my hope:

1. that you—all you non-Indians—study and learn about our systems of thought and internal social and scientific practices, leaving your Patriarchal Anthropology and History textbooks, academic training and methodologies at home or in the closet on a dusty shelf.

2. that your faculties, conference organizers, community organizers stop giving lip service to including a "Native American" for this or that with the appended phrase: "if we only knew one!" Go find one. There are hundreds of resource lists or Indian-run agencies, hundreds of Indian women in organizations all over the country—active and available with valuable contributions to make.

3. that you will strongly discourage or STOP the publication of any and all articles *about* Indians *written by non-Indians,* and publish work written by Indians about ourselves—whether you agree with us, approve of us or not.

4. that you will *stop colonizing us* and reinterpreting *our* experience.

5. that you will *listen* to us and *learn* from us. We carry ancient traditions that are thousands of years old. We are modern and wear clothes like yours and handle all the trappings of your "civilization" as well as ours; maintain your christianity as well as our ancient religions, and we are still connected to our ancestors, and our land base. You are the foreigners as long as you continue to believe in the progress that destroys our Mother.

You are not taught to respect our perfected cultures or our scientific achievements which have just recently been re-evaluated by your social scientists and "deemed worthy" of respect. Again, let me re-state that 150 years of bad press will certainly make it extremely difficult for most white people to accept these "primitive" achievements without immediately attempting to connect them to aliens from outer space, Egyptians, Vikings, Asians and whatever sophisticated "others" you have been educated to acknowledge as those who showed the "New World" peoples "The Way." Interestingly, the only continents that were ever "discovered" (historically) where people already lived are North and South America. Who discovered Europe? Who discovered Africa? Who discovered Asia? Trade routes, yes—continents, no. Manifest Destiny will continue to reign as long as we teach our children that Columbus "discovered" America. Even this "fact" is untrue. He actually discovered an island in the Caribbean and *failed* to discover Cathay!

When we consistently make ourselves aware of these "historical facts" that are presented by the Conqueror—the White Man—only then can all of us benefit from cultural traditions that are ten to thirty thousand years old. It is time for us to *share* the best of all our traditions and cultures, all over the world; and it is our duty and responsibility as the women of the world to make this positive contribution in any and every way we can, or we will ultimately become losers, as the Native Race of this hemisphere lost some four hundred years ago.

Photograph by Diane Reyna

Doris Seale

His Half-Breed Wife

She was so quiet
Nobody noticed her watching
All those years housebound
      —or nearly—
The wind in the grass an enticement.
Only her eyes gave her away;
They were little grey birds
In cages.

The day she went was strange enough.
Somehow
We didn't find her.
Doubting it was just the wind
That called her,
I'd rather not walk out alone.

Merry Harris

Real People

We were Real People
Long before TV stole name
Of our ancestors.

Green Corn Festival

Golden corn ripens.
Houses swept clean,
Dance begins:
Green Corn Festival.

Nila NorthSun

stories from the res.

getting a loan from the bank
they ask
do you have collateral?
old mose says
what's that?
they say
a car?
no
a home you own?
no
furniture?
yea yea
got a whole houseful
tables chairs bookcases
nightstands dressers
everything
they say
very fine
old mose gets loan
defaults
they come to get furniture
houseful of fish crates.

somebody broke into
his house last night
they took his t.v.
radio rifle &
scope

they even took
his mouthwash?

laughter on the res.

Linda Belarde

Precious Bits of Family

Some memories stand out
sitting in the kitchen
canning fish smoked in our smokehouse
with Mom, Aunt, sisters, cousins
Listening to the news of the first moon landing
Telling Gramma that yes, there're men on the moon
but we can't see them.
She looks puzzled
as if we are crazy
but listens politely
as nice people often do to crazies.
The berry-picking trips
dreaded because everyone else was on a picnic
turning into our own picnic
with crackers and soda pop and blueberries
and laughter over who ate more than they picked.

Mary TallMountain

My Wild Birds Flying

Sources: *Novel in Progress,* There Is No Word for Goodbye
TallMountain Journal, excerpts October 1976-Summer 1978
Letters of Clem Stroupe

Novel in Progress:

Little more than a hundred miles below the Arctic Circle where the Yukon el-
bowed south, it carved vast curves into the earth and enmeshed itself within a
sinuous maze of lakes, creeks, and swamplands scattered with stands of spruce and
cottonwoods; there, birds nested in spring—slim dark marsh hawks glided low
across the ponds, pale gerfalcons brooded in the tallest trees, ospreys hurtled from
snags of dead alders to return with fighting silver sheefish, a lone peregrine plum-
meted out of the eye of sun for an unwary mallard—all searching out their quarry:
snowshoe hares browsing at dusk on new willow buds, teal flinging up out of glassy
sloughs, fat ground squirrels scuttling for cover, and the smallest birds and rodents,
new-spawned sockeye salmon hidden under clouds of mosquitoes, and black gnats
among the blowing reeds: a great echo chamber of drumming and hooting, whistling
dives, low croaking and gargling, shrieking rushes halted by feathery explosions;
this was the Kaiyuh, ancient Indian hunting grounds. Now deserted winter camps
huddled sparsely in immense sweeps of land. It was the time of *Ggaaɫ,* the king
salmon. The Indians were gathered into the heart of their country.

Lidwynne's family camped on the river four miles north of Nulato. They had
come here since all the bands wandered in winter through Kaiyuh and returned to
the river for the time of *Ggaaɫ.*

Up the bank, Mamma and Auntie Madeline's heads in bright bandannas bobbed
and nodded. The glittering crescent blades of their *tlaamaases* slashed straight
along shining cellophane bellies of immense fish. Pink strings of eggs slithered into
squat tubs. Salmon dangled in crimson curtains between old silver-grey posts. Thin
blue threads floated out of the smoke house. Away toward the meadow stood a
row of brown weathered tents.

West, where the land lifted toward the hills, bears came in summer to bumble
in the bushes for ripe blueberries. When salmon were running, black bears lum-
bered down to the water and hooked them out with thick sharp claws. They were
small but fast and dangerous. The elder persons warned the children never to go
away from camp alone. Bears might get them. Woodsman might. They called him

173

Nik'inli'een. Nobody knew anything about him except he had an animal's head, teeth like a saw, and paws as big as dishpans. He'd carry you off and you'd never be seen again.

When she heard that, Lidwynne had run to the tent right away. Mamma was sitting on a wooden box. Her hair fell to the edges of the box and she was combing it with *bitłee* Daddy Clem had given her. *Bitłee*'s brown and gold streaks flew through the black hair. Mamma passed her hand slowly over Lidwynne's cheek and she felt the coolness of Mamma's skin and the warmth of the sun. She almost forgot what she wanted to ask Mamma.

"Oh, *eenaa*, what's *Nik'inli'een*?"

"Pretty girl!" Mamma cried, hugging Lidwynne and laughing with her happy sound. "There's no *Nik'inli'een*. Just don't you run off from camp, that's all." She pushed Lidwynne's round stomach softly. "Go play!"

At four, Lidwynne was a chubby little girl, fast stretching out taller. Her eyes were round black berries reflecting the sun. Her dimpled hands were grubby. They looked like fat Christmas cookies as she carefully patted Mamma's hair. Mamma kissed her and the hair came down all around both of them in a curtain.

Lidwynne ran back to the other children. "You're crazy," she shouted. "There's no *Nik'inli'een*! My mamma said so."

Mamma would never tell her a lie.

TallMountain Journal
San Francisco   October 1976

Again I saw the white curtain blowing inward, in the window. What old memory is quickened when I see that recurrent fragment?

Letters, Clem
Phoenix 1976

I earned my little old fiddle by selling frilly red satin Ladies Hose Supporters. Jass got his guitar working in the hops and I found a young feller down by the railroad tracks with a beat-up Cornet. He taught us both the clarinet. We played for country dances around Hoptown when Jass and I were 12 and 15 years old.

First time I saw your Mom was when I was practicing my fiddle for a dance there in Nulato village. Your Mom dressed in nice little frocks she got from Sears, and wore her fine black hair bound around her forehead with bright bands of cloth. When I came to Nulato, she was taking care of her Papa and brothers, and like a few other women did wash for some of us soldiers.

It was a tight little village and was controlled by the Littlebuck family. Taria was a Littlebuck. After Mary Joe married him, she was tangled in that family, but her own family favored us whites. The Littlebuck folks didn't like that. It caused lots of fights between the two of them, and Taria was mean and stubborn. He got to beating up on her, and before I got there she finally slapped him with a dried fish and drove him out to Kaltag for good. She told everybody she was done with him, Littlebuck or not!

The Littlebucks were medicine people for years back. Sophia Littlebuck certainly had a weird hold on all the Nulato people. And that would account for so many of the eerie happenings in Nulato that year of 1921, and even further on in time.

I'd never been overboard about any woman. Friends, yes. Love, no. I had small orchestras in California towns, had fun playing for dances, but I never fell for any girl. Then I met your Mom. And oh, your Mom was beautiful. The old folks in the village who knew everything (that's why they stared out their windows) scolded your Grandpa for letting me come to her cabin at night (altho I don't think he ever knew it). She lived in that culture, it held her fast, and she had to do things you'd never dreamed.

It was the greatest part of my life. I was tough as a wet walrus hide. Outdoors most of the time. Some days on the trail the dogs and I were lost in the black, and my leader Moose always found the right trail no matter how deep buried. Then without warning that year when you were three, and as though a dark curtain dropped between us and reality, the tragedy of that Fall slammed into our lives. Even the kids felt the mysterious spirits that hovered among us. The people talked of omens. I looked for meanings in the very shadows. All of it is written relentlessly in my memories.

First your Mom got TB, and then the Doc and his wife wanted to adopt you kids. The upshot was, I lost all three of you at one time. I thought I ought to go Outside. It seemed like the only way right then. So I did, and kicked around out there, did some railroad duty with the S.P., played a little with bands. The War was over, and through the grapevine I heard you had married and died in Newfoundland. It knocked me for ten miles galley-west. I signed up for a new tour of duty in Seward. This was years later, in 1938, I married Grace Harshman. And she was paralyzed in Hawaii during the first of World War II, by poliomyelitis.

I cared for Grace all my life after that. And sometimes when I looked back on the past, it sure as hell seemed like we'd all been zapped by some spirits, way back there in the '20s.

TallMountain Journal
and Novel in Progress
June 1976

Rex Twohill saw me off on a Western 437 at noon over a city veiled in a bank of fleecy fog underpinned by steel. The flight was humdrum, and did not change until we deplaned at Anchorage to board a regular Wien flight for Galena. I found a lot of Alaskan faces among the many white ones. At Galena, the ratio swung to a preponderance of native faces. Out on a six-seater Cessna south to Nulato, I saw the Kaiyuh Mountains east, streaked with glaciers white against the slopes. A moose stood in a small lake still and alone. From the plane he was so small, a deep black Rorschach blot. The trip was surprisingly short, and I had just got caught up in the immensities of river, land, and sky when we began circling for Nulato. Steadily we swooped down above the village's galvanized roofs gleaming back the sun in sharp oblong shapes. Graveyard Hill approached, disappeared under us, and the dun-colored clay of the airstrip rose. We jolted across the rubbled cement tarmac to a slow hiccuping stop.

The river flowed past sometimes red, sometimes grey, and now, still getting rid of the glacial loess, was roily and full of silt. It pushed impatiently against the banks. Salmon have been seen at Holy Cross downriver, but still linger below till the river goes down. People are getting whitefish and sheefish. Summer coming on, they are friendly, and everybody laughs, sometimes self-consciously.

Across Mukluk Slough, Clem's old radio transmitter tower lies crooked after fifty years' decay, a black and rusty ruin.

Cousin Elmer: Shy, beautiful piercing eyes. He mourned about his drinking and angrily said he must stop it and go out to Anchorage and support his wife and little girls. But, he growled, it was so hard to leave Nulato. He didn't see how he could live out there. He said, "When I knew you were coming my heart got tight." He pounded his chest. Sometimes he wept, staring out over the river.

Grey clouds brought rain from the north. It is so gentle I walk down to the river. It speaks very softly to me. Swallows dive and soar from the mud nests under the eaves of the convent of Our Lady of the Snows. Now about fifteen of them swoop down at once, fly in a perfect oval low above the river, dart to the sky again.

Rain drummed on the iron roof all night.

The island is closer than I remembered. It is overgrown with alder and willow and now a long sand spit has built over the years. Kids swim there in summer. I had seen it in my mind shadows far away and dusty blue. Mary Joe used to fish behind it. I wonder if she sometimes met Clem there . . .

Tassie Saunders made a picnic for us at Graveyard Hill. The old graves were peaceful in the hot sun. We forged our ways around and around through the scratching brush, reading the carved names on the white crosses, visiting people gone, and felt the loving, kind presences. We ate Spam and graham crackers high above the river beside the Demoski grave houses, and she said long ago, Koyukuk warriors attacked the Russian fort at Kaltag and massacred all but a little boy who escaped on snowshoes. In his old age, he was buried just across the river under a lonely spruce tree.

We knocked mosquitoes off each other and talked for several hours in the shadows of swaying rosebushes. In front of us a wild rose in full bloom trembled in the wind.

We didn't find Mary Joe's grave.

I grieved a while, then she said, "Your Mom is in there," and tapped her finger against my chest. At last I realized. It didn't matter where my mother was laid. I would have her always, in there.

TallMountain Journal
June 25, 1976

I am immensely weary. Due to the constant daylight of the time of the Midnight Sun we go to bed at 2 or 2:30, in the morning, no earlier, and are up nevertheless by 7:00 A.M. So many people, so much talk, so many conflicting stories. My brain is exhausted.

Their language is atrocious. They talk very fast. Each has terrible discrepancies. And I suspect lies, to mollify me, because they know I'm searching for Mom and Billy's graves. They peer out the windows of the cabins. Nothing is hidden. (The Honey Bucket is the greatest leveler in the world!) The only relaxed people appear to be the Anglo teachers. The natives and their kids are easily hyped. It's culture shock.

Paula and Sister Anne Eveline say I've idealized the people too much. I agree. They aren't poor, they have too much, and they suffer from it. They drink and lie and steal and they have lost my mother's grave.

Cannot write, need aloneness, have got these notes together with tremendous difficulty. Weariness, disillusion, communication breakdowns. I think they resent my staying with Sister. And probably they're saying that I'm a white woman. What's the use?

At Kaltag, Missouri Stanley is suspected of drowning his own brother. Someone told me that to explain the people's dislike of him and his little wife, Anastasia. Someone else said, "He sleep with his daughter in beaver season. Now he look like beaver." No one helps them. Missouri is bent over with age and rheumatism and perhaps some ancient paralysis; Anastasia is frail and bloodless and totally dependent on him. They can't fish because nobody will carry anything up the bank for them.

Novel in Progress

Now I feel that I have done some strange unknown thing I came here to do and it's done and I must go on.

A gale is blowing and the river is filled with whitecaps. The trees back by the playfield are boiling with wind and the three spruce trees by the greenhouse are bent nearly double by the lashing wind. Water dances on the tops of the brilliant blue oil-drums. Rows of young cabbages inside the fenced convent garden are whipping tender new leaves. Hunched-over people hurry by on the river road. I hear the wind mourning where the swallows nest; and I remember the sound. *Niguudzaagha* visited me once more before I went away.

CRAZY DOGHOLKODA

Wind from the river warm on our backs,
birds bustling blue from nowhere.
What time is it? We did not care.
In Nulato there is no time
in the summer of midnight sun.

Why are they here? these caches,
huddled in rows like sad old men,
their faces silver grey.
What do they hold that the robber hours
did not filch from them yesterday?

The logs were rich with years of salmon
kept safe since the walls were new.
Heavy snows had slanted them west,
Winter would topple them
in the end.

Niguudzaagha moved. Always he moved
like a drifting log.
"You think we should pull them down?"
His look was ebon-dark.
I shook my head.

"Oh, sure, we got new ones.
But we keep these. This bunch I built
when I was just young."
Shrugging lazy, he shot
a jet of chew
brown to a hummock of grass.

"That one," he rumbled, "one time
we put in biggest bunch of K'odimaaya
anybody ever trap.
Those ones over there. We stay in there
that winter our *yah* burn down.
This one, *eeto bito'* die in here."

We sat and watched a while.
When it was time to go, he got up.
"Onee'," he said, face warm as the sky.
"Crazy old *dogholkoda*, hah?" he growled,
looking over his shoulder.

dogholkoda	caches
k'odimaaya	muskrat
yah	house
eeta bito'	grandfather
onee'	come on

The cold pierces the walls and the heat from the brittle iron stove does not last. The lovely chime of Father Baud's handwrought grandfather clock doesn't overcome the howling gale. The flung velvet of the island can't outweigh the dirt that blows in the road. The spirits in the graveyard can't show me where my mother lies; and I will not let them persuade me to return here. But I know who I am. Marginal person, misfit, mutant; nevertheless I am of this country, these people. I have used their strengths. I have wrestled to the earth their weaknesses that have echoed in me.

But I must find another home. This one is not what I sought.

TallMountain Journal
July 1, 1976

Singing at evening, the dogs make strange music. They are cowed, somnolent, tied up all summer around their dugout pits where constant raking of their claws has marked the dirt. In winter they are powerful and majestic, and speak of the age-old alliance between men and dogs.

One old lady's son set up a fish cutting table for her, back of their cabin. She told me, "I wish he put me up a tent too, so it be like fish camp." The elders live great stretches of their lives in the Old Time.

As cousin Mary Walker said,

"Oh, they loved their land. Their life, that land. One time we were having meeting below the Kuskokwim somewhere, and there were non-natives there to talk to natives about the land and the elders told the white people. "WHEN YOU PEOPLE NEED SOMETHING, YOU GO TO YOUR BANK TO GET YOUR MONEY. AND US, WHEN WE NEED SOMETHING, WE GO TO OUR LAND. THAT'S OUR BANK."

Mary Rose cooked a big haunch of moose Monday, with all the fixings. She put it out on the table and it was all gone by the next day. Everyone eats whatever is out on the tables. As I was visiting with her family, in Kaltag, she was celebrating in a mild way every day I was there, cooking and putting food out, people dropping in all day long to eat and talk and learn the news. That's the hospitality of Alaska, of the people.

TallMountain Journal
July 3, 1976

Cousin Edna had a potlatch and brought out a skin scraper my Mom had used until her death; my grandpa had made it. The handle was a warm smooth brown wood, silky with years of use. I held it in my hand and felt it. I knew it was designed exactly to her grip, my mother. She had used it, and now my hand held it. The only article I have touched that she used.

It didn't occur to Edna to offer it to me, though she must have seen the longing in my face. And I would not ask for it. I said secretly: Let it stay here. It belongs here and it will be here when I have joined Mom. I have far more than a scraper. I have her, I have Mom, her blood and her spirit.

Tassie has the blues. Her husband died last year; this is her first fish season without him. She hasn't been fishing or cut fish. Her mind dwells on death; she rushed to find her baby hawk, fearing he was dead somehow. I can't remember how many deaths she told: Drowning of a little girl by two teenage boys; stabbing of an eighteen-year-old girl by an older boy; a man caught in a motor and chewed up by it, his body lost in the river; more stabbings; the death of a boy from sulfa pills with whiskey; her grandpa's death by falling with a thud while driving dogs. He hit a hollow and—"I guess his heart drop down," she adds. Then just a week ago, the GI drowned near Galena, found by my cousin Freddie Ben while setting nets 100 miles south at Kaltag, the GI swollen to the size of a log. All this within the space of just a few months.

Mosquitoes are so sluggish they cloak our shoulders and heads. The river is like glass and there is no wind. The people look at me with eyes of the past. They watch every move of my hands on the china, the fork, the food. The rain is starting (the mosquitoes knew it would) and there is no sound but a dog far off stirring his mates into a wild wail in the half-night.

My roots are here, I feel them deep in my memories, in the hidden spaces of my blood. It doesn't matter where I live; I will see the rounded cabins set together. I will see the hill where my mother lies clean and shining under the roots of this ground.

Across the river a streak of red dirt turns copper all along the bank of the island, and the river burns with the lowering sun in bronze flames. A seagull wheels above, looking for salmon. I will fly over Graveyard Hill at morning on one of Harold's bushplanes.

Janice Gould

An Oregon Story

In gray rain, October or November,
it was morning where I lived on the farm.
Early, after chores, that Yakima woman
drove up the road to my place on the bluffs.
She had come to pick me up.

She was sure pretty, that woman.
She had a wide face, obsidian eyes,
and hair the color of blackbirds' wings.
She had long legs, and every guy
at the cannery where we worked
was a fool for her. But it was me
she took home to meet her kids.

Maybe her husband was out hunting
with his pals all weekend long.
I never saw him but once, on Saturday night,
when he came home, changed clothes,
and went out to the bar
carrying his shoes in his hand.

She waved goodbye to him
not bothering to get up.
She went on smoking and said,
"Sing some more."
So I threw back my head
and sang 'Your Cheatin' Heart'
in a way Patsy Cline would have understood,
and the Yakima woman said,
"That was real good.
Do you want to go to bed?"
She didn't mean with her.

I slept on the sofa, she slept alone
in a thin chemise.
The kids slept scattered
all over the floor.
About four in the morning
I got up and looked at the sky.
It was not relief to see it
so cold, clear and full of stars
above the black fir forest.

Janice Gould

The Caves

I.

It is late afternoon
and we are on the edge

of a mountain where light falls,
firing the bowl

of this old volcano and the burnt
slopes of grass.

Today we are not in love,
so our words take

the shape of crows and fly
off in different directions.

Longing, I feel, or regret,
watching their departure.

II.

Her hand has convinced her
I am here when

it rests on my neck
and her cool fingers,

unsteady with desire,
twine in my hair.

III.

Shadows cross the earth
where I stare at the cold

mulch of leaves and twigs underfoot.
There are caves up there,

she says, pointing above us,
where Indians would go at night

seeking visions, listening for songs.
There are burn marks

where it looks as if torches
flared against the rock ceiling.

Do you want to see? she asks.
I answer, no.

Barbara Cameron

Wild Turnips

The phone rings. "hi, may I speak to Barbara?" "yes, this is she." "oh, hi Barbara, I'm calling because we would like you to speak at the rally this weekend."

The phone rings. "hi, may I speak to Barbara?" "um, this is Barbara." "Barbara, great! I finally reached you. How are you? How you doing?" "oh, I'm a little tired. My job is in its monthly stress time and I've been working weekends and I'm..." "oh gee, that's too bad. Would you be willing to..."

The phone rings.

I've been biting my fingernails again. god, what an annoying habit. My hair is too long and the cigarette smoke at work is starting to smell delicious. I've been staring at the phone at work. If the 08 or 99 lines light up, they could be for me. Well after all, I can say no or that I'm on a long distance phone call, tell them to leave a message or eat cake. I could use an old Catholic trick, say three hail-marys and four our-fathers. Then maybe no one will call me today to ask me to do something for them. These past weeks have been frustrating because it seems that I'm excessively in demand at work, in the community. And I'm messing up at home. NO ONE, I repeat, NO ONE has looked me in the eyes and asked me softly or even loudly, How are you? How are you? And the persons I call to ask to have a quiet drink for a few hours are at meetings, running to meetings, study groups, in their own space—need to be alone. Yes, maybe we can get together in a few weeks. We all begin to sound the way a jolly green giant packet of green beans cooks. 1-2-3 instant, presto quick food, quick conversation. In two minutes or less, let me tell you how I am. There is little nourishment in jolly green giant green beans. In my night dreams, I'm at the same physical location for weeks. The ocean. Many nights we're hiding bodies or escaping from marauders. Other nights I'm at huge rallies— waiting for something to happen. Then one night it does—I contract with the gay latino alliance to be their hit person in assassinating a south american dictator. Our planning is superb but we panic, I panic. I wake up heart beating fast. In the daytime, downtown from 6th street to embarcadero, I pretend I'm at a pueblo and that there is a sky, there is piñon burning somewhere, burning somewhere.

Imagine that I have an inner life. Imagine that I sleep, laugh, do simple things, make love twice, three times a day, buy flowers for Linda and toys for Rhys, play jokes and tease tenderly.

IMAGINE, IMAGINE . . .

Autumn is dried corn stalks in a field. I am there. The sky is blue endless, endless. Pheasants run through the stalks—surprising themselves with their noises. The leafless trees bring chill in the morning. I am there too. Bluejays sing to ripe mushrooms in the moist woods. I am there. The snakes are curled asleep, the nests are empty—the clouds come later to make grey days leaving no shadows for geese overhead. Autumn. I am there.

Winter. Winter. You can find me there—in the skies—northern lights, illusive, shimmering, disappearing—light upon light—there, there in the sky—I am—snow falling wet and it too disappears. Inside—inside—seek refuge. It is warm—a simmering stew on the wood-burning stove—I am there—the steam rising—sweet-smelling, settling on window panes, quietly, quietly—creeks run smooth under ice.

But no—lightning strikes the ground fast—brilliant and clear—creates static too. I am there. Crackling—jagged and dangerous—above, the thunder—I am there, I am there. Swirling, power that is awesome, strong, loud, rumbling sky and earth. Sunset in summer over mountains is purple red blue gold pink and then dark is night. Snakes travel in pairs, so do I—sleep when the sun is high, bringing dry winds, give you no comfort. I am there on hills where wild turnips grow—stop—be certain that is wild turnip you dig—not its deceptive sister growing close—fooling you, fooling you. Summer, summer is hot drenched rocks, I am there.

Springtime—I am there—the meadowlark—first bird to sing—bringing you messages—listen, listen, I am there—far off wild animals stir, bears, prairie dogs,even coyotes get happier—I am there—the warm spring breeze ice melts above eagle soars—I am there—soft green grass and delicate bark—springtime.

Eager wait the shale cliffs along the creek—smooth wet rounded pebbles—dig your hands in, squeezing, digging deeper—pushing along its wetness, fingertips want more. I am there—sliding rolling toward dark moss on banks—I am there, sand bars exposed—waiting for creek ripples to leave more grainy sand—smooth, waiting, waiting, I am there.

I am there—find me—see me—know me—in your dreams—in your quiet moments—when you sit alone by the river—thinking—find me—see, I am there—when you're scared—when you're angry, just before swollen tears fall—I am there. I am there—sweet sage is burning—cleansing the air.

reservation girls

we've got some
tough girls here
one when she was 12
shot her girlfriend
who didn't want to play with her
she hasn't shot anybody else since
but she stabbed a boyfriend
in the arm
another girl fought older kids
when she was in grade school
now at 30 she takes on
tribal council members &
white girls in cowboy bars
this other girl got into
5 fights while she was pregnant
two of them were with her
250 lb. husband he knocked
a couple teeth loose
3 fights were with long time rivals
& even though they kicked her in the
stomach
she ended up the winner
chasing them down the road
another girl loves
a good fight
& beats the shit out of anyone
who happens to look crooked at her
while she's drinking in the indian bars
tough girls
& they want to be my friends
i suppose it'd be better

than being their enemy
but how can you have a good time
drinking & carrying on
when you know at any moment
they might knock you off the barstool?

Salli Benedict

Sweet Grass Is Around Her

A woman was sitting
on a rock.
I could see her
clearly,
even though
she was far away.
She was Teiohontasen,
my mother's aunt.
She was a
basket maker.
When I was young,
my mother told me
that her name meant,
"Sweetgrass is all around her."
I thought that it was a good name
for a basket maker.
She was in her eighties
now.
She was short like me,
and a bit stout.
She knew the land well;
and the plants,
and the medicines,
and the seasons.
She knew how to talk
to the Creator too;
and the thunderers,
and the rainmakers.
She had a big bundle of sweetgrass
at her side.
It was long, and green,
and shiny.

Her big straw hat
shaded
her round face,
It was very hot.
She pulled her mid-calf-length dress
down to her ankles,
over her rubber boots.
She brought her lunch
in a paper bag;
a canning jar of cold tea,
fried bread,
sliced meat,
and some butter,
wrapped in tin foil.
She placed them carefully
on the rock.
She reached
into the bag,
and pulled out a
can of soft drink.
I thought it strange.
She didn't drink
soft drinks.
Then,
she reached for her
pocket knife.
Basket makers always
have a good knife.
It was in the pocket of
the full-length
canvas apron,
that was always
safety-pinned to her dress.
She made two sandwiches,
. . . looked around
Saw me looking at her.
Her eyes sparkled,
she smiled.
She lifted up the soft drink,

and signaled me to come.
After we ate,
she stood up
on the rock
and looked out.
She smelled the air.
I knew that she
could smell the sweetgrass.
I never could.
She pointed to
very swampy land.
Mosquitoes, I thought.
I was dressed poorly.
We didn't talk much
but we could hear,
and listen to each other.
She never forced me
to speak Mohawk.
Mohawk with an
English accent
made her laugh.
She didn't
want to hear
English though.
We would spend
all day
picking sweetgrass.
Sometimes
we would look for
medicines.
One time,
my mother asked her
what she thought
Heaven would be like.
She said
that there was sweetgrass everywhere
and people made
the most beautiful
baskets.

Drawings by Jaune Quick-To-See-Smith

SELF PORTRAIT

© JAUNE QUICK-TO-SEE SMITH 1984

Emilie Gallant

White Breast Flats

As one grows older, and the past recedes swiftly as a bird, wings extended in the wind, there are people and places whose contours, caught through the clouds of memory, take on the dimensions of myth. For me, one such place is White Breast Flats on the Piegan Reserve in southwest Alberta where the plains give way to the foothills, the Rockies loom near, and the great obelisk Chief Mountain stands power-fully at the entrance to northern Montana. White Breast Flats is a name known only to a few. My grandfather, Otohkostskaksin (Yellow Dust), was the one who told me that name, and recently, when I read the name in a book, I felt a special joy. Seeing it in print, so many years and miles later, seemed to establish the place as fact, and it opened again for me the pages of that precious time in my past.

White Breast Flats was occupied solely by my grandparents, and on occasion by my mother. It was located on the first bottomland north of the Old Man River on the west end of the reserve, and the land that rose behind it—the valley wall I suppose you could call it—reached its highest point there, a half-mile from bottom to top, two miles in span. That valley wall was laced with a maze of foot-trails, and there were bushes aplenty of saskatoon, whiteberries, gooseberries, chokecherries, and bullberries. There were also wild turnips and cactus berries there. All of these berries gave nourishment to my sister, to my brother, and to me as we played or just wandered through.

The bottomland stretched from the base of the hill towards the river for a mile and a half at its farthest point and a quarter of a mile at its closest. The one-roomed log house my grandparents lived in was situated about a half a mile from the hill and about two hundred feet from the river. The Old Man has probably eaten away the spot where the house stood, for the bank crept a little closer each year. The trees there were of several varieties, but other than the willows, cottonwoods, choke-cherry, saskatoon, and pussywillows, I am still unable to name the trees that made up the forest. Where there were no trees, the grasses grew wild and rampant, and I can still see fields of yellow and white sweet clover and the ever-present and ven-omous purple thistles which stabbed at us with their thorns every chance they got.

We were brought up to fear bears; and although I never saw a bear while I was growing up, I was always on the lookout for the one which I was sure was wait-ing for me to relax my guard. The most fearsome thing I ever saw was a snake. I was afraid of water; and the river bank we clambered down to reach the green, swirl-ing currents was dotted with holes which I thought were the homes of deadly and poisonous snakes. My sisters were both strong swimmers and enjoyed swimming across the river, but I would churn inwardly with fear as I watched them splash and drift away, bantering and yelling with abandon. And there I would be, standing first on one dirt-caked rock with a dried-up water spider stuck to it, and moving to another, sometimes walking in the water up to my knees very cautiously and carefully, for the rocks were slippery. Sometimes a fish would awake and swim off suddenly, making my heart jump and my throat constrict with a scream I held in. The river was a malevolent thing to me, never friendly. I watched warily for the mythical water-being which I was convinced lived somewhere in the greenest, deepest part. It had to. Otherwise, where did all the foam come from which flecked the river's surface; it had to be the water-being's spittle.

One particular day, I was standing on the river's edge again, watching my two sisters, whom I resented and admired for their fearlessness, when I slipped and fell into the water. It was in the evening and the sun's last rays had turned the river into a golden, glinting, and somehow not so perilous place. I imagined that the water below the surface where the water-being lived was illuminated. In a matter of minutes the warmth of the day was exchanged for the coolness of the evening. My skin was prickled with goosebumps from the chill, and I decided to put on my cotton dress until the two mermaids left the water. I picked up my dress and almost died with fright! A big snake slithered out of my dress. I screamed, and my mother, who had been washing and rinsing clothes some distance away, came running, and I got to ride her piggyback all the way home. I even had her throw my dress in the river, something I always remember, for we were very poor and could ill afford to throw clothing away.

There were plants that my grandmother would collect for her medicinal and everyday purposes. She would hang mint to dry in bunches from a line tied across the length of the room, close to the ceiling. I loved the smell of it, and although I didn't care for mint tea then, I do now. It's not only the taste that I enjoy; it's the remembering of moments of my childhood. Every so often I happen upon a cup of wild mint tea, and the bitterness of it, if the tea is made too strong, brings me back to my mother's house when I was probably five or six years old and deathly ill—or so I remember, because my grandmother was summoned. She was a medicine woman and had in her possession all kinds of herbs and roots with which she brought back to health anyone who was ailing. She came into the house on a cold, winter day, bundled up with shawls and blankets. The snowy wind whipped the log house until chinks of the limestone plaster were peeled off and swept away in the storm. My mother kept plugging up the cracks with rags to keep the snow from being blasted inside. The wet snow that stuck to my grandmother's wraps hissed as it hit the stove. She carried a flour sack, and from this she took out a bag made from fawn hide, spotted and with the little hooves on it. Inside the bag she had wrapped still other small bundles, and she took out something greasy and rubbed my chest. On top of that she placed a layer of dried leaves. Ritually she spat on these, and covered the leaves with a hot cloth. She gave me a drink of an awful-tasting brew, and I wouldn't have drunk it if she hadn't been the one to give it to me. She then chanted holy songs, her voice a little frail and weak at first but gaining strength and fullness until the sound was a soothing prayer. She had a sacred rattle made from rawhide and painted with red ochre; this she shook in time with the cadence of her voice. She closed her eyes as she sang, and as I watched her I saw that she had painted her face with the red ochre, and the hair that framed her face was tinted with it. After her song, she prayed that my health be restored and I be blessed with a long and happy life. From a little buckskin bag rubbed with the sacred red ochre, she took some paint that had the consistency of uncooked pastry but which became oily when rubbed in her hand. This she rubbed on my face and then she left, leaving some brew and plants for my mother to administer to me. She also left an orange in plain sight that I could have when I was well enough. Oranges during the Second World War were rare, and not seen unless at a feast.

Sometimes I can detect the smell of sweetgrass when there is none around. I've grown to know that it is only my grandparents coming to visit me. Sweetgrass—an appropriate name for a special plant. Sweetgrass is the incense the old Indians used to honor the Creator, and the burning of it was a daily occurrence in my grandparents' home. Each morning my grandfather would get up and make the fire in the stove and as soon as the warmth made getting up comfortable, my grandmother would rise and they would pray together. He would burn incense to greet the Creator, to give thanks for life and health of family and friends, and to ask for guidance in living the day, as well as for help in some special need. Then they shared a song between them and a smoke on their pipe from chunk tobacco.

A quarter of a mile east of the house and just where the woods began was a spring. This was where my grandfather got our drinking water. He used a wooden stoneboat to haul it. The stoneboat was constructed of two logs at the bottom; they were the runners, smooth and heavy. On top of them were wide planks of board, bolted onto the logs. The planks were so old, I used to sit and scratch them with my fingernails and a papery, powdery substance would come off the wood. Grandfather would hitch up the team, and we children tagged along, jumping on and off the stoneboat with our dogs barking happily behind us until we reached the spring. He tied the team to a tree above the spring and carried two pails to bring the water back to the old metal-girded wooden barrel. He would make twenty or thirty trips until the barrel was full, and then he would put a canvas cover over it and tie the cover on with a rope. Once the water was brought home, my grandmother would have a drink of it first, then set about to making a pot of tea.

A slow-moving stream which leaked off the river and eased by the spring was a refrigerator for butter, meat, and the seasonal garden vegetables. The vegetables came from my grandfather's garden at the base of the hill. Everything grew in abundance there: carrots, rhubarb, turnips, onion, radishes, lettuce, potatoes, and sugarbeets. It was neat and ordered, with its straight rows and well-tended mounds of earth. It was fascinating to watch the steam rising from the garden after my grandfather watered it or after a rainfall or shower. I thought a mysterious creature, perhaps a cousin of the water-being, inhabited the earth, and the steam was its breath just as the flecks of foam in the river were the water-being's spittle. I never hung around the garden alone.

The stream that adjoined the spring was the home of a thousand minnows. We would catch some in a jar and take them home, and although we fed them flies and bread, they always died. Long-legged water spiders glided silently around the stream and the little frogs of grey, green, or brown jumped noiselessly, even when they landed in the water. Only our big, clumsy dogs would ruin the silent stream with their panting, lolling tongues as they splashed in, sitting right in the water to have a drink. Then they would shake their wet bodies mightily until it seemed as though it was raining. Our shouts of anger and surprise would usually result in their jumping on us with friendly licks and muddy paws. Surprisingly, of all the dogs we had (it seems they were all shaggy) the only one I remember is Pete. Pete, the short-haired hound with long legs, a tail like a whip, and shiny ears, one of which would sometimes get stuck inside out or underside up, was blacker than the deepest badger-hole we dared to peep into, and he had white, laughing teeth and a rosy, wet tongue.

There was a faded, creaking ghost house on top of the hill. It had two stories and no windows or doors, just openings from which whitemen ghosts watched passersby. It used to belong to a white man I knew only as Inopikini, which means Long Nose. We would go to the ghost house in broad daylight, always in the protective company of my mother and grandmother. The wind was always blowing through the house, flapping wallpaper, rattling floorboards, shingles, and window-casings. It was a wonderful, mysterious, scary place to go poking around in. It had lots of rooms, small ones and big ones. There were old curly shoes, clothing of all kinds, pieces of furniture, bits of toys, stray dishes, cracked cups without handles, and faded pictures still in their frames. We never took anything, because then Inopikini would haunt us until we returned what we had taken, or else, if he was a real mean ghost, he would twist our faces.

There was a trapdoor in one room which we never dared to open because we were sure something stayed down there, but we would stomp across it, each one stomping harder than the last but always with mother or grandmother in the room. After we verbally challenged the ghosts who had the guts to come out and meet us face to face, we would climax our visit by scaring only ourselves and stampede off in hysterical screams, our bodies prickling and our eyes wild with fear, not daring to look back lest we see Inopikini hot on our trail.

I always expected to see a tall, emaciated man with hair all over his skin and blood around his nostrils and perhaps little horns growing out of his head. He was always garbed, in my imagination, in the cracked, curly boots he left in his house and his body covered with the rags scattered about through the rooms.

Summer reminds me of my grandmother mashing cherries in her tipi, which was erected as soon as it was warm enough to sleep outside. My old grandmother used to herd us up the hill to dig for turnips and pick berries for some upcoming feast, but those were the times we wished berries didn't grow. It was always a hot day when we yearned to be down by the spring and we quarreled amongst ourselves and sneaked away.

On hot summer days when I wearied of playing or had nothing to do, I would go and ask my grandmother to check my head because it was itchy. She would put aside whatever she was doing and check my head, all the while telling me stories until I fell asleep. Sometimes when I didn't fall asleep soon enough for her, she would tell me to erase a cloud by rubbing my hands together and concentrating on that cloud. I demolished many a cloud. My grandmother was a tireless old woman who never rested. She was always busy beading, fixing deerskins, fixing berries (drying, mashing, sorting), repairing clothing, cooking, sweeping, washing clothes and minding us kids. She would gather wood on a big piece of canvas and carry it home on her back or drag it behind her. Then she would sit at the woodpile and chop wood with her hatchet, which she also used for butchering the deer my grandfather killed.

I haven't been to White Breast Flats for a long time now, too long. The log house and outer buildings have long been dismantled and carried away for firewood, and the paths and roads are overcome by weeds. Only the descendents of the magpies, gophers, rabbits, and frogs have reclaimed their ancestral grounds. Perhaps a rusted wagon-wheel or a skeletal hay-mower tells a hanging eagle that people once lived here. White Breast Flats will not happen again; it only lives in the longings and hearts of Ippisuwahs, Piiksi Kiipipi Pahtskikaikana, and Itsinakaki, the grandchildren whose voices once rang clear and echoed through its secret places.

Nan Benally

Rug of Woven Magic

I remember
  you weaving your beautiful rug
    by the kerosene lamp.

Your hands
  deftly moved
    among the strands
    mystically creating
      a design that slowly evolved
      with each row.

Sometimes I would come
  to visit
    while you were gathering
  those special herbs
that transformed each skein of
carefully carded wool into
    hues that only nature provides.

Patiently
  you would answer my questions
  "What plants are they?",
    "Where do they come from?",
      "What are their names in English?",
          ". . . in Navaho?"

I envied your knowledge
  of all that was mysterious
    to me.
You were the
  magician that created
    rugs so beautiful from
      seemingly very little.

Your weaving
    spoke a language of its own
        that needed no interpretation.
All the magic,
    all the beauty
    had already been transformed
        through you.

There are many legends
    that you have told me
        (as you sat at the loom)
    of how things came to be.
As I listened
    the rug seemed to take in
    all that you spoke.
You become a part of
    what you made,
        for in it was
    your beauty,
        your wisdom,
            your pride.

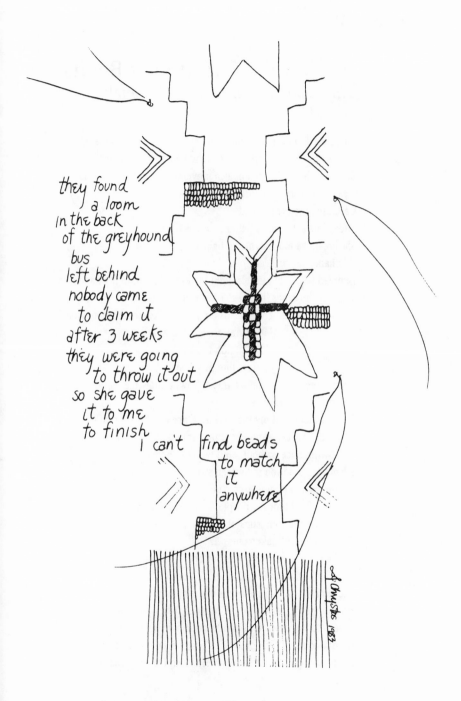

they found
a loom
in the back
of the greyhound
bus
left behind
nobody came
to claim it
after 3 weeks
they were going
to throw it out
so she gave
it to me
to finish
I can't find beads
to match
it
anywhere

Elizabeth Woody

"You Smell Like Grandma's Beads"
The lesson I caught from the smell

There used to be a long silent end of hall,
Enticed by the secrecy, I walked the length to watch her.
Beading, she sat tangled in arm movement. Center only, one hand
Steadying everything through the night.
Carefully, the beads lined
into colors gathering a pattern.
She created a movement, set tightly.
(My hands in her beads.)
Jumbled string, old jewels, light buckskin caught in my hand treads
smelling the beads, breezes of her womanness.
   She said, "Moccasins for you . . . Fourth of July is soon.
   Moccasins are good to wear.
   You shouldn't forget how they feel
   on days like July Fourth."
Strange the answer seemed then. Now, I know the tension
that provoked her answer.
Twice I thought of my moccasins. Once as a little girl at feast
watching my feet. Another at my Grandfather's funeral.
Once with, once without, both with Grandma.
Silently go beads on my waxen string,
my life contemplating each stitch.
   "I fight for my people . . . I need a scalp
   for the coup stick of my group.
   I haven't taken one yet."
   "Take mine. I won't be needing one," I thought.
   "Not yours! A blonde one I need."
Everything you told me needs understanding.
I remember what was told in jumbles, like beads unstrung.
A bead to put down for Grandma somewhere in there . . .
It's odd to smell Grandmother's beads inside someone else.
My hands running over the patterns again, asking questions.

Oddly, I smell in another grandchild, quietness
that needs some stitching to be done within him.
Perhaps by himself, it'll get done.
Grandma and Grandpa collected their children.
In the careful years, they made things good to know on days
like this. Fighting the battle still waged against us.
In the siege, tightly I bead myself. The light stretches down the hall,
moves in the night to make good feasts once more.
Old people say, "This life can't last forever. Money will run itself out."
The war is silent. In the quiet hours of womanhood, I am taught to prepare.

Dorothy Hayes

A Short Autobiography

I remember most of my childhood as a bad nightmare. My mother was a person I never understood or—try as I would—I couldn't get along with her.

I loved my grandfather very much. He was a Cherokee Indian. He came from the Ozarks & his people were poor dirt farmers. He worked his way thru medical school as a boxer & waiter, etc., & became a well known Doctor in St. Louis, Mo.

When I was five years old, I contracted Polio. I was not able to walk for years afterwards. I had surgery at Shriners Hospital & from a wheelchair went to braces & crutches & by the time I was 15 years old, I was able to walk without their aid. I also had a speech defect which was corrected at "Elias Michael School for Crippled Children."

As I got into my teens & even before that, I felt different & left out of activities from the other kids.

I was forced to go to a "Normal?" school when I got to 6th grade, as they said it would be good for me to learn to be with "Normal?" people. From then on, I quit learning anything & did not *try* to learn. The only subject I cared for was art. Kids made fun of the way I walked & climbed stairs & I had a real inferiority complex & hatred of them.

When I was in my 3rd year high-school & 16 years old, I started going to low taverns on skid row in St. Louis.

My mother would come with 2 plainclothesmen & have me put in a place for incorrigible children but this didn't stop me. I played Hookey from school & ran away from home twice but I was a Juvenile & they always brought me back. The only thing that hurt me in that time was my grandfather seeing me drunk.

When I was 18, I left home for good. I went to another city, got a job in a law office. (I managed to graduate from high school somehow.) I drank every nite after work & soon lost my job. There was a succession of jobs but my drinking increased steadily. I met a soldier & married. I worked & still drank every nite. The marriage lasted 2 mos. & I went to Chicago. I was 19 yrs old by this time. I had some idea of attending art school but it never materialized. I had numerous jobs, worked in offices and finally in bars, because I could get all the drinks I wanted there. I could never handle my liquor & got in trouble a good deal with the law when I drank. I had many Indian friends & I seeked them out in their bars to drink with. None of them seemed to be able to handle their liquor & hit the bottom fast. I had a deep resentment inside of me against white people, although, I am half white and I secretly hated them. When I drank, this took the form of violence. I married again. An Indian man I met in Chgo. & we had 4 children. After 5 years, this marriage also broke up, with my wrecking our apt. in a drunken rage. I was put in jail & my mother took 2 of my children & 2 were adopted. When I was released from jail, I found another neighborhood to drink in. Madison St. in Chgo. It was skid row. I hid there from my husband (he finally divorced me.) & my mother & family. I learned to drink wine & take pills. I almost got into hard dope but something stopped me, I don't know what. Probably the thought of the money a habit like that one would take each day. I learned to be a thief, and panhandler. Many nights, I slept in doorways & woke up covered with snow & half-frozen to death. I got in trouble with the cops many times & I would always try to fight them when they wanted to lock me up. I would do *anything* to get pills & booze. I was in State Hospitals & County Hospital & had many falling accidents. When I was 37 years old I went into the DT's at County Hospital. I was in there because gangrene was setting into my fooot. I had gone to a doctor to try to stop drinking & he had given me parmaldehyde & I didn't take it like it was prescribed but took the whole bottle & got parmaldehyde poisoning. They were going to amputate my foot but again, something saved me. I spent 14 years on Skid Row. Most of it is like a dream to me now & I don't know how I survived it but I did.

By this time I was 39 years old & on Welfare & walked with a cane. I had attended A.A. many times before for short periods & slipped. But I went back again to meetings. I stayed dry 8 mos. I couldn't give up my pills in this time. I drank for 4 more years. In this time, there were a series of Hospitals, nut-houses & jails. I beat up a woman that lived in the same bldg. I did & almost put her eye out. When I went in front of the judge & she was there accusing me with her face all bandaged, and I remembered nothing. It was all a blank to me as it had been lots of times before when I got in trouble over something I did while drinking. Again, I had to go to jail—not remembering the crime I was accused of. I was on a cane & the matrons told me I didn't belong there—"House of Correction" or "Bridewell"— & I agreed with them. I thought in those days I was losing my mind & I belonged in an Insane Asylum.

At 42 I again tried to stop drinking. I would sober up a while & then drink again. I was never able to give up my tranquilizers & sleeping pills at any of these times.

I then went to work for the Salvation Army, & after 14 mos. realized that somehow I had been able to stay sober. I decided after 20 years to go see my mother & family. We had been corresponding for about a year. They were in California.

I came for a visit & saw my 2 grown daughters. They were both married. My mother asked if I would like to live here & I moved out to California.

Things weren't really different between my mother & me but one of my daughters & I became good friends. I found that she & her husband were heavy into dope & they went on a vacation & were asphyxiated by a hibachi while sleeping. I felt terrible guilt & I drank again after this & was very ill. I drug myself back to AA, tried to build my life back up again. This time I pulled myself away from the pills also. This was hard, for now I really had to face reality. I had to break off all relations with my mother & family & start out again in a new and unfamiliar place. I started going to M.P.C. 4 semesters ago & took some courses in Art & guitar. Then I got into Chris Moore's Clay Class & began to make figures. I love the work. I also continue with the guitar lessons at school. I have substituted new interests for old ones. For the first time in my life, I have some Peace of Mind! I am learning to live with the bad days as well as the good ones & when some problem arises, I don't bury it in drugs of some kind. I have found out most people aren't so bad if you like yourself a little bit. I have acquired some self-respect & I can respect other people too. I only live one day at a time.

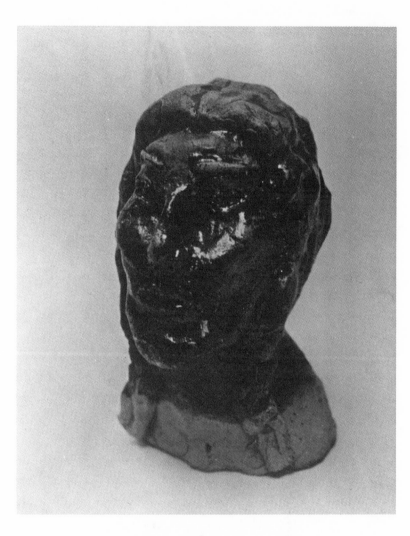

Woman's Head by Dorothy Hayes

Margot LeBrasseur

A Song for Healing

a touch from my hands brings you strength
hey-ya o hey-ya
the cries from my heart take away the pain
hey-ya o hey-ya
Now you will get better, stronger
                              Yo!

Geraldine Keams

Canyon Day Woman Blues

Woman VII (Ester)

Alcohol Counselor,
Indian Woman,
Mother.
Married to an alcoholic,
Indian man
Father of two.
Mother wants out.
He feels sorrowful,
Tired.
She feels defeated.
She sees the sadness in
the young son's eyes . . .
"Mommy, I'm hungry."
She sees a small beam
of light.
Suddenly realizes, her husband
will never change.
Can't babysit a grownup
man no more!
"I'm leaving him!"
Confidently, positively,
She smiles.
A feeling she hasn't had
in a long time.
I listen to Ester.
I think,
Right on,
Navajo woman,
Right on!

Wendy Rose

Well you caught me unprepared

Well you caught me unprepared

beached like driftwood, pink against beige
in the evening sun, ivory bleached
after all the bluster of your storm.

I am counting all my fingers and toes,
taking stock
of what you took. Can it all be
pushed back together
with glue, tied up with a thread
leaving only the memory
of thin seams, a scar
where your kiss
was blown away?

I turn each bone carefully
this way and this way,
examine and stretch, measure
the hope or the lie
all the gods gave us that
pain is a vitamin
to make us grow.

This is last summer's wreckage here
no different, but now each movement
is cautious, men more dangerous.
The friends that are left grow old,
release the bloom and let seeds fall
sterile to my ugly hands.

I am sure you have it
precisely figured
these latest of nights
in ghostly books; you must have
surveyed and compiled
whole nightmares of literature.
This one is a history.
I am preliterate again, an egg,
an infant, now
the toddler pushed underwater
by the green-eyed brother.
Now I am six
proudly pointing off fingers,
expanding the measured length of self
against couch cushions and puppies
suddenly larger than
all my years.
Now I am twelve
bleeding between the legs,
thirteen now with blood-caked hair
and bullet holes beginning
between my eyes. Sixteen
sound asleep in the scream
of police sirens, eighteen curled up
in the arms of doctors, nineteen never
stop grinning, chained
to the glamor of speed.

Twenty years it takes to ask
if it matters how dark my skin,
how slanted my eyes, how hung in beadwork
my earlobes and neck. Twenty-one
I surround him on his Honda
in the mountains. Twenty-five
on hands and knees, bandaged and skinny,
leaving him again and again.
Thirty the weather turns tropical,
palm trees and flowers are a dance
in the city. Thirty-four I am counting
the storm wrack washed up
on my thighs, testing elbow and fingers,
toes and lips, pulling strands of hair
silver against black from my mouth
where the wind has strung them like seaweed
or like just the sea.

I skim the bottom of the water now
another beach calling, another
earth in my blood. The songs are swallowed
as fast as I sing them, the muscles aching
with the cost of barley promises.
I am still convinced no matter what
that I am stronger than any storm.
Every song straining against the shackles
I creep the ocean floor and don't believe
anything about me can drown.

Kate Shanley

Thoughts on Indian Feminism

Two years ago, after the Ohoyo Conference in Tahlequah, Oklahoma, the Ohoyo Resource Center put together a book titled, *Words of Today's American Indian Women: Ohoyo Makachi*. Among the addresses included is Rayna Green's speech, "Contemporary Indian Humor." A mixture of anecdote and tribute to Indian women, Green's talk addresses with humor the serious problems facing Indian women in America today. Of the relationship of the Indian women's movement to the majority women's movement, however, she writes:

> Many people want to know why the Indian women's movement didn't really join the majority women's movement in this country. I've come up with a new theory of why they have not joined the women's movement. You've all heard that one of the first things people in the movement did was to burn their bras. I've decided why Indian women didn't do that. Being the shape most of us are in, we were afraid they'd have to bring the fire trucks in from ten miles around. So you can understand why we were reluctant. We figured we stopped air pollution in Eastern Oklahoma by not doing that kind of burning.

Aside from the obviously funny reference to the large-chestedness of Indian women, Green plays off the popular mistaken notion that "the first thing" feminists did to protest women's oppression in this country was to burn their bras — a weak, if not self-trivializing gesture — and she jokingly cites bra-burning as the point where Indian and "majority" women depart from each other. Of course, humor is humor — and what could be worse than taking a joke seriously? Then again, what could be more foolish than denying the serious assumptions that underlie most humor, assumptions as commonly-held beliefs. The American women's movement historically has been and continues to be more than a weak protest against the notion of woman as sex symbol, but the questions remain: why do Indian women seem reluctant to join the majority women's movement? Or do they?

Toward the end of the 1983 Ohoyo Indian Women's Conference on Leadership, I began to notice that the participants were not referring to themselves as feminists, although the group of women present are as strong and committed as any group of women in America today who are working for change. Why, then, do Indian women avoid the designation "feminist?" The more I thought about it, the more that question began proliferating into many questions: how many other women (of all colors and creeds) have I encountered in my travels (plenty!) who do not choose to identify as feminists? What do they have in common with Indian women? What is a feminist, anyway?

My thoughts on the questions raised thus far by no means represent a consensus among Indian women; in fact, before I could begin to deal objectively with the subject of Indian feminism, I had to come to terms with my own defensiveness about representing other women, particularly other Indian women. On the one hand, I am a woman who refers to herself as a feminist. If most Indian women do not refer to themselves as feminists, does that fact make me somehow *less* representative, *less* Indian? On the other hand, does the theoretical feminism of the university constitute something different from (though, perhaps giving it the benefit of the doubt, correlated to) the "grass-roots" feminism Ohoyo represents? To some extent I know that I suffer the conflicts of an "academic squaw" (to borrow a term from poet and educator Wendy Rose), a certain distance from the "real world."

Attending the Ohoyo conference in Grand Forks, North Dakota was a returning home for me in a spiritual sense — taking my place beside other Indian women, and an actual sense — being with my relatives and loved ones after finally finishing my pre-doctoral requirements at the university. Although I have been a full-time student for the past six years, I brought to the academic experience many years in the workaday world as a mother, registered nurse, volunteer tutor, social worker aide, and high school outreach worker. What I am offering in this article are my thoughts as an Indian woman on feminism. Mine is a political perspective that seeks to re-view the real-life positions of women in relation to the theories that attempt to address the needs of those women.

Issues such as equal pay for equal work, child health and welfare, and a woman's right to make her own choices regarding contraceptive use, sterilization and abortion — key issues to the majority women's movement — affect Indian women as well; however, equality *per se,* may have a different meaning for Indian women and Indian people. That difference begins with personal and tribal sovereignty — the right to be legally recognized as peoples empowered to determine our own destinies. Thus, the Indian women's movement seeks equality in two ways that do not concern mainstream women: (1) on the individual level, the Indian woman struggles to promote the survival of a social structure whose organizational principles represent notions of family different from those of the mainstream; and (2) on the societal level, the People seek sovereignty as a people in order to maintain a vital legal and spiritual connection to the land, in order to *survive* as a people.

The nuclear family has little relevance to Indian women; in fact, in many ways, mainstream feminists now are striving to redefine family and community in a way that Indian women have long known. The American lifestyle from which white middle-class women are fighting to free themselves, has not taken hold in Indian communities. Tribal and communal values have survived after four hundred years of colonial oppression.

It may be that the desire on the part of mainstream feminists to include Indian women, however sincere, represents tokenism just now, because too often Indian people, by being thought of as spiritual "mascots" to the American endeavor, are seen more as artifacts than as real people able to speak for ourselves. Given the

214

public's general ignorance about Indian people, in other words, it is possible that Indian people's real-life concerns are not relevant to the mainstream feminist movement in a way that constitutes anything more than a "representative" facade. Charges against the women's movement of heterosexism and racism abound these days; it is not my intention to add to them except to stress that we must all be vigilant in examining the underlying assumptions that motivate us. Internalization of negative (that is, sexist and racist) attitudes towards ourselves and others can and quite often does result from colonialist (white patriarchal) oppression. It is more useful to attack the systems that keep us ignorant of each other's histories.

The other way in which the Indian women's movement differs in emphasis from the majority women's movement, lies in the importance Indian people place on tribal sovereignty — it is the single most pressing political issue in Indian country today. For Indian people to survive culturally as well as materially, many battles must be fought and won in the courts of law, precisely because it is the legal recognition that enables Indian people to govern ourselves according to our own world view — a world view that is antithetical to the *wasicu* (the Lakota term for "takers of the fat") definition of progress. Equality for Indian women within tribal communities, therefore, holds more significance than equality in terms of the general rubric "American."

Up to now I have been referring to the women's movement as though it were a single, well-defined organization. It is not. Perhaps in many ways socialist feminists hold views similar to the views of many Indian people regarding private property and the nuclear family. Certainly, there are some Indian people who are capitalistic. The point I would like to stress, however, is that rather than seeing differences according to a hierarchy of oppressions (white over Indian, male over female), we must practice a politics that allows for diversity in cultural identity as well as in sexual identity.

The word "feminism" has special meanings to Indian women, including the idea of promoting the continuity of tradition, and consequently, pursuing the recognition of tribal sovereignty. Even so, Indian feminists are united with mainstream feminists in outrage against woman and child battering, sexist employment and educational practices, and in many other social concerns. Just as sovereignty cannot be granted but *must be recognized* as an inherent right to self-determination, so Indian feminism must also be recognized as powerful in its own terms, in its own right.

Feminism becomes an incredibly powerful term when it incorporates diversity — not as a superficial political position, but as a practice. The women's movement and the Indian movement for sovereignty suffer similar trivialization, because narrow factions turn ignorance to their own benefit so that they can exploit human beings and the lands they live on for corporate profit. The time has come for Indian women and Indian people to be known on our own terms. This nuclear age demands new terms of communication for all people. Our survival depends on it. Peace.

Debra Swallow

Keep a Dime

Broken Treaties, FBI, What civil rights?!
Trials, Convictions, Appeals, Courtrooms, Truckstops,
    Holiday Inns
Endless highways, two bottles of No-Doze
Phone call, phone bills, another pack
    of Marlboro Reds,
Sleeping bags, legal pads,
    (gotta write tomorrow's press release)
Organizing rallies, slide shows,
Speaking forums, pow wows, feasts,
    giveaways, wars,
Another pot of coffee—make it to go
    please,
Only 80 more miles, who brought the
    banners, signs, flags, literature,
    posters, pins?
Mailing lists, donations please, we have
    a struggle to continue.
Gas money, postage, air fare, cab fare,
    printing bills.
Gotta score a tipi, a coleman lamp and batteries
    for the $200 portable stereo.
Teach the children and their parents the
    1868 treaty and Leonard Peltier, the IRA-BIA
    and summer's 49's.
Make a bustle and a roach and
    don't forget the deerhide guncase.
Spend your money on the movement
But keep a dime for the phone,
    it's worth a lawyer you know.
Women's work is never done.

Luci Tapahonso

A Breeze Swept Through

For my daughters, Lori Tazbah and Misty Dawn

The first born of dawn woman
slid out amid crimson fluid streaked with stratus clouds
     her body glistening August sunset pink
       light steam rising from her like rain on warm rocks
         (A sudden cool breeze swept through
         the kitchen and grandpa smiled then sang
         quietly knowing the moment.)
She came when the desert day cooled
and dusk began to move in
in that intricate changing of time
     she gasped and it flows from her now
     with every breath   with every breath
     she travels now
        sharing scarlet sunsets
        named for wild desert flowers
        her smile a blessing song.

And in mid-November
early morning darkness
after days of waiting pain
     the second one cried   wailing
     sucking first earth breath
     separating the heavy fog
     she cried and kicked   tiny brown limbs
     fierce movements as outside
     the mist lifted as
     the sun is born again.

(East of Acoma, a sandstone boulder
split in two—a sharp, clean crack.)
She is born of damp mist and early sun.
She is born again   woman of dawn.
She is born knowing the warm smoothness of rock.
She is born knowing her own morning strength.

Marcie Rendon (Awanewquay)

this woman that i am becoming

this woman that i am becoming
is a combination of the woman that i am
and was
this journey backward will help me
to walk forward

Sister
the rape of a woman
is the rape of the earth
the rape of a child
the rape of the universe

as i voice these words
i watch you turn your well-kept
sunday morning presence
from this body that is heavy
with emotion
surviving
i have violated
your myths of motherhood
knowing full well
some silent summer night
my daughter's screams
will invade your
peaceful sleep
as they echo off the stars
some dew-covered morning
you will walk outside
to gather strawberries
and find instead
a gaping cavern
the ultimate rape
having finally been committed

Sister
hear me now
let us take this
journey together.

Excerpts from Letters

December 10, 1982

Dear Ms. Brant,

Greetings of peace. I hope my words finds you happy and content upon all your paths of living.

As you can see from the above address, I am incarcerated, as a matter of fact I have been sentenced to die. I stand innocent, but theres no justice in white man's courts. I have much knowledge of the law. But I cannot have faith in any courts, that sentenced me to death, for a crime I never had any part in.

I'm of Cherokee blood, from North Carolina. I also have a little white in me. I've been raised in white man's world and was forbade more or less to converse with Indian people. As my mother wanted me to be educated and live a good life, free from poverty. I lived a life of loneliness. Today I am desperate to know my people.

Ms. Brant, I would appreciate any thing you can or will do, that will aid me in my need of my people.

Thank you for any and all concern to my words.

I, remain

Raven

Dec. 14, 1982

Dear Raven,

I was so happy to get your letter. It made my day very beautiful.

Please tell me more about yourself. I was very moved by your letter. It seems that so many of us have missed out on our own heritage. My family is Mohawk but education was the highest goal, and it was hard to not assimilate. I am not educated. I got married when I was 17. My three daughters are grown up now. I am 41, no longer married, am a feminist and a lesbian. I began writing about 2 years ago, and now feel like I can do my political work in this way. I am poor, but live in relative freedom. I have received many letters from my sisters in prison, and I am struck by the mobility and freedoms that I have. I admire your courage and you are all an inspiration to me. I am honored and blessed that you will be contributing to the issue. Thanks for writing. Nah weh.

Beth

December 19, 1982

Dearest Beth,

Greetings sister; peace and love.

Thanks for the letter, cards and stamps. I really appreciate you taking time and concern for me.

I admire you greatly. You are of freedom. I seek friendship of those who know and accept themselves, and stand in truth, with-out plastic covers. I salute you!

I've been in this tiny cell for 11 months. I do not have visits. My "white" family ignore me. I do not call them or bother to write. Each of them live in the world of booze & drugs, my half-sisters and half-brothers have very little going for them. I do not hate them. I understand them. They are not my people, "they are white."

I was hurt at first, but I've worked myself up from this emotional level. I do not want more hurt. I find it hard to believe that all people are mean and cruel.

Beth, I value your opinion greatly. I think white people are lying evil monsters. They have no truth, love or honor. My Grandfather taught me the red man is wisdom and loyal. Is this correct? I am as my Grandfather taught me, that I should be and I do get hurt often, but my dealings with Indians is rare, as my mother wanted it.

Beth, I am giving serious thought to asking the state to drop my appeals and set a date for the gas chamber for me. I do not want a life sentence or to fight years of appeals. The state says I killed a elderly lady. I won't even kill a dog. I am so ashamed by this. I'm in this cell 23½ hours a day. I have my radio to keep me comfort. I read a lot and exercise. I'm into keeping my body agile and firm. As my mind I will not allow to stagnate, I work both body and mind. I thirst for knowledge. I've read all the books here on Indian people. I sketch a lot. I am a loner.

You are in control of your life and self. I'm so thrilled to meet someone who is there own person. Its important to me, how people are. I do not bend in my values to please others who disrespect me.

Thanks for the ear. I guess I needed to rap. I guess I consider you a-ok.

The best to you sister.

May all your dreams come true, and peace be ever constant with you.

Thanks for listening to me.

Walk freely sister.

        peace and love

        Raven

Dear Raven,

Thanks for your wonderful letter. There are so many things to write to you, so many words to share.

Yes, I do know myself, but often hate that woman. I am proud to be an Indian, proud to be a lesbian, but have to constantly fight the hatred, the desperation. My people hate me because I'm a lesbian. Whites hate me because I choose to identify with being Indian. It is a vicious circle, one that never stops.

I would like to know more about your life. Do you remember much from when you were a kid? I lived with my Grandma & Grandpa until I was 12. They wanted so much for all of us kids to be successful and educated. I never finished high school. I got married when I was 17. It was 1959 and I was pregnant. There wasn't much of a choice. Abortions were dangerous and illegal and besides that, much too expensive for the likes of us. So I married, had three daughters, finally threw my husband out. He abused all of us.

Sometimes I *do* think that all white people are evil. But my mother is white and some of my blood is hers. I have spent too long hating myself, and I don't want to anymore. My lover is white. She comes from a poor Polish family. She understands so well. Probably because she was raised so poor. She knows what it is like to be despised and to be ashamed. I have several women friends who are white. I love them. The difference is that they work very hard to understand, to speak out against the racism and classism that exists. We are not supposed to talk with each other about important things. We are supposed to assume and to hate. I want to stop that in myself. I used to think that only Indians were good. But that is not true. None of us has escaped the hatred and racism heaped on us by the elite few. I believe that we will act out the negative things expected of us. My uncle was a drunk. He didn't start out that way. He certainly didn't want to be one, but he became the stereotype expected of him by whites. I loved him very much, although he hurt many people, my Grandma especially. I truly believe that white man hates and craves what is inside those of us who are colored. They envy our connections to the spirit, to the earth, to a community, to a people. Because they envy that; they hate us, and will do anything to get rid of us. So all the things . . . slavery, genocide of Indians on this continent, as well as in Latin America; the Holocaust, missionaries in China, the Vietnam War . . . all of these a calculated program of extermination. And I add to that, the millions of women burned at the stake centuries ago, because we were women, because we were lesbians. As long as we don't make the connections between us, we are lost and will be played by white man. I am sending you a book called *This Bridge Called My Back*. I think you will understand everything. It was written by women like you and me. Indian, Black, Latina, Asian. It is a book that made a great change in my life.

What I want to say is that I'm frightened much of the time. I may never know what it is like to be in prison. But I have been in a mental institution, unable to get out, unable to go to the bathroom without asking. Unable to stop the harassment by the nurses, by the orderlies. Unable to stop the drugs they shoved down my throat. When I refused to eat, they stuck needles in me to feed me. They threatened me with shock treatments, with insulin therapy. There was a point where I had to decide to live or to die. I chose life for myself. At that point I didn't know why I did. But now I know I am needed for something. I would never have known you. And I am blessed by knowing you. So perhaps there is a reason for choosing life over death. I am your sister. I will listen to you. I will be on your side.

Stay in peace, little one. I am thinking of you. Nah weh.

Beth.

Jan. 6, 1983

Dearest Beth,

Greetings: my sister and peace be with you. Thank you for your very beautiful letter, and the stamps.

Enclosed please find a article done on me. The photo sucks, but then they always show the worse ones. Very little of what I said was printed. I asked them to state why my lack of faith in the maryland court system was so bad, but as you can see they didn't. I say I am innocent, and if the courts can convict a innocent person, how can I have any faith in the same court system.

I only wish to be free of this place. I'm dieing slowly. I need to feel the earth under my feet. This place resembles a tomb. I'm sealed away from the things that make living, living. I need fresh air and space to move.

I often ask the guards to bring me a cup of fresh air, in a joking manner. Some of the guards here are real people. Thats not a odd statement even though it may be hard to understand.

Beth, thank you for entrusting me enough to speak to me of your pain. I surely agree, white men both hate and envy us. How can they not. We are strong, we can relate to the earth, while they cannot relate to themselves! I should think, rather than be envious, those ones should seek knowledge and learn our ways. But to do this, they would have to accept Indians as wise. Our bonds are different.

I do not think much about this up-coming event [the execution]. I simply await it. My dream would be to have a medicine man with me and a couple of my own people.

I just had a hour with a female reporter for the paper. I'm drained, but I believe she was sincere. She says she will print the true me. I hope she does.

Well, my sister, as you can see many changes have taken place in my life. I do not know how I feel. I'm only confused and tired.

I think of you often and how well balanced you appear to be. But as you spoke to me, you are fearful also. I surely understand you are as me. I do not let my fear to show and rarely admit I have any fear. With you I feel comfortable. I do not fear your rejection of me in my true form. I've grown more since I wrote you last. I've accepted myself more and I've looked at myself from all angles. For the most part, I like what I see.

I feel like a child who is undressed in public. Many people asking questions, but printing falseness.

Dear sister I will conclude here and get some rest of body and soul. Stay in peace.

Love, Raven

Jan. 26, 1983

Beth,

Greetings may your peace be great and your paths smooth. Beth, the article you have and all the others have not printed my words.

All these articles that I've seen say that I want to die because I can't stand this place. But the articles don't say that I say I'm innocent and do not have faith in the same court system to free me, that gave me death, when I'm not guilty. Its not so important that people know I wish to die, but it is important that the reasons be brought to life. I can die easier for a cause, when I walked into that courtroom, I was as naive as the rest, but my sister I'm proof of the corruption. The next time you or one of yours could be here. We need to kick these people back. I do not trust anyone. I talk to you. My lawyers do not contact me at all. They are poor excuses for lawyers.

I know how reporters like to write about our pain, but they print lies. For example the Jan. 24 *Time* article.

Many christians write, but I do not believe the way they do. They are really weird sometimes. I usually ignore them. They only want to save my soul. I need to save my life.

These church people speak on many things that I do not believe is any of there business. I got into an argument with the chaplain here. He says I shouldn't smoke and he talked of homos (his word). We got into a heated rap. I'm not into women, or at least, I haven't been, but if I am or if I'm not, I do not feel he should judge. What difference does it make whom we love??

I hope you are ok my sister. Let me say if I should have to die, I shall be as brave as anyone can be. But somehow the country just should be aware of this lousy justice system.

I shall keep you in my thoughts. Take good care of yourself special one.

Love,
Raven

Joan Shaddox Isom

Tremolo

A woman is making the tremolo into the wind
No longer is it the song she once made
For her husband and sons in battle
Now
She sings it for herself
This woman is a strong woman
Her face is etched in lines
That have not yet made an ending
In another time she would be called "man-hearted"
But now she has turned her back to the wind
and the four winds take her cry and carry
it to the four directions, to all-women
And her tremolo is a new song
She sings in a voice of rolling thunder
Saying,
Listen, women! The new word for *strong*
is *"Woman-hearted!"*

Karen Cooper

A Native Woman – 1982

Living in the air
Landless
I pretend the floor
Is ground.

The only earth I visit
Is the dump
Asking Mother to forgive
My trash upon her face.

Time in its metered regularity is irregular
I do nothing that is natural
I have even taken the moon's control from my blood
My children are strangers
My family is back "home"

I am alone—
Landless
9 to 5
driven by bills to pay,
and a car to feed.

I am a Native Woman
I have that much
It's more than most
I am not ignorant
I know what life should be.

Pencil Self-Portrait by Rosemary Anderson

Anita Valerio

I Am Listening: A Lyric of Roots

There is the cab driver root and elevator
root, there is the water
root of lies   The root of speech hidden in the secretary's
marinated tongue   There is the ocean
root and seeing
root, heart and belly root, antelope
roots hidden in hills   There is the root
of the billy club/beginning with electric drums   Pale
cubicle lanterns hang over infants' foreheads   root of
embraces
   There are lines I see
   in my hand when I open
        my palm   There are telephone
poles strung all over and feverish
roots of glass
     onion root   tall tale
        root of hunters   smoky
ascensions into heaven   trails
        beat out of ice   There is the root
of homecoming   The house my grandfather built first   I see
him   standing in his black
hat beating the snake with a stick
        There is the root shaped
by spirits speaking
in the lodge   There is the root you don't
want to hear and the one that hides
from you under the couch   There is the memory root—hidden
under blankets   The root of space camouflaged a curtain of
silk   surrender   Root of teeth and
the nape of the goat   oranges, fog
written on a camera   There is the carrot owl hunting
for her hat in the wind   moccasins
     of the blue deer
  flashing
in the doorknob

                    There is the guitar root flushed with musical
ants   billboard
root glowing root
of lard and syrup   interchangeable roots of heaven and hell
Picasso shrimp hidden in ceiling
cracks   There is the root of sex eating
pound cake in the kitchen   crumbs
                                        crumbs
                                                alibis
crumbs
a convict astroprojects   She is
picking up her torches, picking up her psalms, her
necklaces

Woman

Woman
   will you come with me moving
      through the river to soft lakebeds
Come gathering rice with sticks
   will you go with me
      down the long waters smoothly shaking
         life into our journey
            Will you bring this gift with me
            We'll ask my brother to dance on it
            until the wildness sings

Selected Bibliography

The books listed below are available from the publisher, or from Turtle Grandmother Books, P.O. Box 33964, Detroit, MI 48232.

BOOKS BY CONTRIBUTORS TO A GATHERING OF SPIRIT

Paula Gunn Allen	*Coyote's Daylight Trip* (poetry), La Confluencia Press
	Star Child (poetry), Blue Cloud Quarterly
	A Cannon Between My Knees (poetry), Strawberry Press
	Shadow Country (poetry), University of California, Native American Series
	The Woman Who Owned the Shadows (novel), Spinsters, Ink.
Marilou Awiakta	*Abiding Appalachia: Where Mountain and Atom Meet* (poetry), St. Luke's Press
	Rising Fawn and the Fire Mystery (children's book) St. Luke's Press
Salli Benedict	*Satkens Tsi Nahoten Seiave* (textbook), Mohawk Language Consortium
	Kenennakekwa Okahra (textbook), Mohawk Language Consortium
	Tsiakostiakwen Okahra (textbook) Mohawk Language Consortium
Elizabeth Cook-Lynn	*Then Badger Said This* (poetry), Vantage Press
	Seek the House of Relatives (poetry) Blue Cloud Quarterly
Charlotte DeClue	Chapbook forthcoming, Strawberry Press
Anita Endrezze Danielson	*Claiming Lives* (poetry), Confluence Press
Diane Glancy	*Traveling On* (poetry), Myrtlewood Press
	Red Deer (poetry), Myrtlewood Press
	Dry Stalks of the Moon (poetry), Myrtlewood Press
Joy Harjo	*The Last Song* (poetry), Puerto de Sol
	What Moon Drove Me to This? (poetry), I. Reed Books
	She Had Some Horses (poetry), Thunder's Mouth Press
Linda Hogan	*Calling Myself Home* (poetry), Greenfield Review Press
	Daughters, I Love You (poetry), Loretto Heights College
Joan Isom	*Foxgrapes* (poetry), Foxmoor Press
	The Moon in Five Disguises (poetry), Foxmoor Press
	Suncatcher (editor; poetry), Foxmoor Press
Nila NorthSun	*Diet Pepsi and Nacho Cheese* (poetry), Duck Down Press
	Small Bones, Little Eyes (poetry), Duck Down Press
Wendy Rose	*Long Division: A Tribal History* (poetry), Strawberry Press
	Academic Squaw (poetry), Blue Cloud Quarterly
	Builder Kachina: A Home Going Cycle (poetry), Blue Cloud Quarterly
	Lost Copper (poetry), Malki Museum
	What Happened When the Hopi Hit New York (poetry), Strawberry Press
Carol Lee Sanchez	*Conversations from the Nightmare* (poetry), Casa Editorial
Jaune Quick-to-See-Smith	*Montana Memories* (illustrator), by Ida Patterson, Salish Kootenai Community College Press
Mary TallMountain	*There Is No Word for Goodbye* (poetry), Blue Cloud Quarterly

Luci Tapahonso   *Seasonal Woman* (poetry), Tooth of Time Press

Anna Walters   *The Sacred* (textbook; with Peggy Beck), Navaho Community College

JOURNALS AND NEWSPAPERS

American Indian Quarterly, Native American Studies, University of California, Berkeley, CA 94720

Akwesasne Notes, P.O. Box 435, Mohawk Nation, Roosevelttown, NY 13648

Blue Cloud Quarterly, Blue Cloud Abbey, Marvin, SD 57251

Contact 11, P.O. Box 451, Bowling Green Station, New York, NY 10004

Coyote's Journal, P.O. Box 649, North San Juan, CA 95960

Eagle Wing Press, P.O. Box 117, Meriden, CT 06540

The Greenfield Review, R.D. 1, Box 80, Greenfield Center, NY 12833

The Indian Voice, 102-423 West Broadway, P.O. Box 8544, Station H, Vancouver, British Columbia V5Y 1R4, Canada

Inuit Today, 176 Gloucester, 3rd Floor, Ottawa, Ontario K2P 0A6, Canada

Native American Directory, National Native American Co-operative, P.O. Box 5000, San Carlos, AZ 85550

Native Self-Sufficiency, Box 10, Forestville, CA 95436

Ohoyo, Ohoyo Resource Center, 2301 Midwestern Parkway, Suite 214, Wichita Falls, TX 76308

Saskatchewan Indian, P.O. Box 3085, Saskatoon, Saskatchewan S7K 3S9, Canada

Sweetgrass, Union of Ontario Indians, 27 Queen Street E., Toronto, Ontario M5C 1R5, Canada

Talking Leaf, 1111 Washington Blvd., Los Angeles, CA 90015

Turtle, Native American Center for the Living Arts, 25 Rainbow Mall, Niagara Falls, NY 14801

Win Awenan Nisitotung, 206 Greenough St., Saulte Ste. Marie, MI 49783

Yukon Indian News, 22 Nisutlin Drive, Whitehorse, Yukon, Canada Y1A 3S5

OTHER BOOKS BY AND ABOUT NORTH AMERICAN INDIAN WOMEN

Bobbi Lee: Indian Rebel (non-fiction), LSM Press

Ceremony (novel), Leslie Marmon Silko, Viking Press

Cogewea, The Half-Blood (first known novel by a North American Indian women), Hum-Ishi-Ma (Mourning Dove), University of Nebraska Press

Coming Out Colored (non-fiction), Maya Chumu, Tsunami Press

Daughters of the Earth (non-fiction), Neithammer, Collier's

Flint and Feather (poetry), Tekahionwake (Pauline Johnson), Paperjacks

Gathering What the Great Nature Provides (cookbook), the People of the 'Ksau, University of Washington Press

HalfBreed (autobiography), Maria Campbell, University of Nebraska Press

Hopi Cookery (cookbook), Juanita Kavena, University of Arizona Press

How I Tan Hides (non-fiction), Katherine Porter, University of Alaska Press

Indian Heritage/Indian Pride (autobiography), Jimalee Burton, University of Oklahoma Press

Indian Women and the Law in Canada: Citizens Minus (non-fiction), Kathleen Jamieson, Indian Rights for Indian Women

In Search of April Raintree (fiction), Beatrice Culleton, Pemmican Publications

Life Among the Qallunaat (autobiography), Minnie Aodla Freeman, Hurtig Press

Me and Mine (oral history), Helen Sekaquaptewa, University of Arizona Press

Mountain Wolf Woman (oral history), Nancy Lurie, University of Michigan Press

Neets'All Gwiindaii (oral history), Katherine Porter, University of Alaska Press

No Turning Back (non-fiction), Paligaysi Qoyawayma, University of New Mexico Press

Pitseolak: Pictures out of My Life (oral history), University of Washington Press

People from Our Side (oral history), Peter Pitseolak & Dorothy Eber, Hurtig Press

Pretty Shield: Medicine Woman of the Crows (biography), F. Linderman, University of Nebraska Press

Pueblo and Navajo Cooking (cookbook), Marsha Keegan, Morgan & Morgan

Shandaa: In My Lifetime (oral history), told by Belle Herbert, University of Alaska Press

Storyteller (novel and poetry), Leslie Marmon Silko, Seaver Books

Tales of the Mohawks (non-fiction), Alma Greene, J.M. Dent & Sons

The Autobiography of Delfina Cuero (oral history), Malki Museum Press

The Life and Death of Anna Mae Aquash (non-fiction), Joanna Brand, Lorimer

The Northern Maidu (oral history), Marie Potts, Naturegraphs

The Ways of My Grandmothers (non-fiction), Beverly Hungry Wolf, Morrow/Quill

This Is the Way We Make Our Baskets (oral history), Dorothy Titus & Matt Titus, University of Alaska Press

Thunder-root (poetry), Judith Volbroth, University of California, Native American Series

Urban Indians: The Strangers in Canada's Cities (non-fiction), Larry Krotz, Hurtig Press

ANTHOLOGIES AND SPECIAL EDITIONS

A Nation Within (poetry & prose), Ralph Salisbury, ed., Outrigger Press

Calyx (special issue of Chicana & Native American literature), Jo Cochran, Diane Glancy, eds.

Carriers of the Dream Wheel (poetry), Duane Niatum, ed., Wendy Rose, illustrator, Harper and Row

The Clouds Threw This Light (poetry), Phillip Foss, ed., Indian Arts Press

Fireweed (women of colour issue)

From the Center: A Folio (broadsides and artwork), Maurice Kenny, ed., Strawberry Press

Frontiers (special issue of Indian women), Linda Hogan, ed.

The Greenfield Review, Joseph Bruchac, ed., Volume 9, Number 3-4

Paper Stays Put (Inuit literature; drawings by Alootook Spellie), Robin Gedalof, ed., Hurtig Press

Plainswoman (special issue by Indian women), Kate Shanley, ed.

The Remembered Earth (North American Indian prose and poetry; large portion by Indian women), Geary Hobson, ed., University of New Mexico Press

Songs From This Earth On Turtle's Back (poetry), Joseph Bruchac, ed., Greenfield Review Press

The South Corner of Time (Hopi, Navajo, Papago, and Yaqui tribal literature), Larry Evers, ed., University of Arizona Press

The Third Woman (poetry and prose by Black, American Indian, Chicana, and Asian American women writers), Dexter Fisher, ed.; Houghton Mifflin

This Bridge Called My Back: Writings by Radical Women of Color, Moraga & Anzaldúa, eds., Kitchen Table: Women of Color Press

When It Rains (poetry), Ofelia Zepeda, ed.; University of Arizona Press

Words of Today's American Indian Women: Ohoyo Makachi (speeches), Ohoyo Resource Center

Notes on Contributors

Paula Gunn Allen: (Laguna/Sioux/Lebanese) Born in 1939 in Cubero, New Mexico. Poet, critic and fiction writer. Her work has appeared in numerous anthologies, including *Lesbian Poetry* (Persephone Press). Her novel, *The Woman Who Owned the Shadows*, will be published in 1983 by Spinsters, Ink.

Rosemary Anderson: (Cherokee) I'm thirty-one years old. Have been a professional artist for sixteen years, and have had my work shown in the U.S. and Paris. I live in Massachusetts with my cats.

Marilou Awiakta: (Cherokee) My name means "eye of the deer." One way women's pain can be healed is by reviving non-patriarchal traditions, which are principally Indian. Feminists (lesbian and straight) have virtually ignored this possibility. I hope for change. I live in Memphis, Tennessee.

Linda Belarde: (Tlingit/Filipina) I was born in Juneau, Alaska. At present, I am the director of the Zuni Learning Center, an alternative high school in New Mexico. I am married and the mother of two children.

Nan Benally: (Navajo) I have lived on the reservation all my life. My poems reflect the cultural aspect of our life here on the reservation in New Mexico.

Salli Benedict: (Akwesasne Mohawk) I was born in 1954, and hold a B.S. degree in Visual Arts and Native Studies. I am the director of the Akwesasne Museum in Hogansburg, New York.

Mary Bennett: (Seneca) I wrote these poems while in prison, serving time for possession of a dangerous weapon. Me and my girlfriend live in Chicago, happy to breathe polluted air. I'm fifty-three.

Alice Bowen: (Navajo) I'm in my mid-thirties. I am originally from Arizona, and currently live in Herron, Michigan, a rural area. We grow our own food, and live in serenity. I have never had my work taken seriously before now.

Barbara Cameron: (Hunkpapa) I was born in South Dakota. I'm twenty-eight years old, a lesbian, and I'm quiet and shy. I live in San Francisco and love cats.

Chrystos: (Menominee) I'm thirty-six and come from wild rice people, from sausage and sauerkraut people. I'm a lesbian with no children, very grateful to be alive, still fighting, still loving, continually changing. I live on Bainbridge Island in Washington State.

Elizabeth Cook-Lynn: (Crow Creek Sioux) I reside in a log home at the confluence of the Spokane and Columbia Rivers. I am a mother and a grandmother, and Associate Professor of Indian Studies at Eastern Washington University.

Karen Cooper: (Cherokee) I'm thirty-six, single mother of two teenage children. I was born in Oklahoma, now live in Connecticut, where I am the director of Native American Studies at the American Indian Archaeological Institute. All I want is to change the world.

Gretchen Cotrell: (Cree Métis) I am a descendant of the Little Shell Band of the Chippewa-Cree. I grew up in the Flathead, in Western Montana. I now live in Long Beach, CA, where I am a social worker in a hospital.

Charlotte DeClue: (Osage) I'm thirty-four and was born in Enid, Oklahoma. I am a wife and mother and now live in Lawrence, Kansas.

Anita Endrezze-Danielson: (Yaqui) I live in Washington State, in the middle of a pine forest, with my husband Dave, and our two-year-old son, Aaron. We have built our own home out of logs. My chapbook, *Claiming Lives*, will be published in 1983 by Confluence Press.

Emilie Gallant: (Piegan) I'm forty-two and a single mother. I was born in Alberta and received my B.Ed. from University of Calgary, Alberta. I am currently at Eastern Washington University, seeking my B.A. in Spanish.

Diane Glancy: (Cherokee) I'm forty-one, a Poet-in-the -Schools for the Oklahoma Arts and Humanities Council. I have my own small press, *Myrtlewood*.

Janice Gould: (Maidu) I was born in 1949 in San Diego, California. I am a lesbian, a writer, and an undergraduate in linguistics at University of California, Berkeley.

Elaine Hall: (Creek) I am thirty-two, born in Alabama. I am a lesbian, I write poems and stories, and I now live in Los Angeles, Ca.

Joy Harjo: (Creek) Thirty-one years old, born in Tulsa, Oklahoma. She is the author of three books of poetry, and currently lives in Santa Fe.

Merry Harris: (Cherokee) I am sixty-one, a semi-invalid. I was given a death prognosis in 1975, but am joyfully and zestfully alive. I have had the example of my Cherokee mother, who was blind and paralyzed, and the example of my Cherokee great-grandmother, who fled into the hills of North Carolina at the time of the Trail of Tears. I live in Ocotillo, California.

Dorothy Hayes: (Cherokee) I'm fifty-two years old, and live in California.

Linda Hogan: (Chickasaw) I'm thirty-five and live in Idledale, Colorado. I have two books of poetry and won the Five Civilized Tribes Playwriting Award for *A Piece of Noon*, produced in Oklahoma.

Joan Shaddox Isom: (Cherokee) I work as artist-in-residence with the Arts Council of Oklahoma. I am the author of two books of poetry, and one of the originators of Foxmoor Press, a publishing cooperative.

Rosalie Jones: (Blackfoot) Born in 1941 on the Blackfeet Reservation in Montana. Received her M.S. in dance from the University of Utah. Studied at Juilliard in New York. Since 1975 has toured in a one-woman dance/mime show entitled "Daystar: A Native American Woman Dances."

Geraldine Keams: (Navajo) I'm thirty-one, born and raised in Arizona on the reservation. Actress, writer, and lecturer. The women I meet seem to echo the strength of the land. They are the heartbeat of the earth and through them survival and struggle are consolidated. I am producing and directing a movie called *A Trail of Pollen*.

Lenore Keeshig-Tobias: (Ojibway) I am thirty-three, from the Cape Croker Reserve in Ontario. I am a single parent, mother of three daughters. I am a feminist and a skeptic. I live in Toronto, where I am an editor for *Sweetgrass* magazine.

Winona LaDuke: (Ojibwa) Twenty-four years old. I'm an author and economist and activist. I live in Massachusetts.

Audrey LaForme: (Mohawk) I'm twenty-nine, born and raised on the Six Nations reserve near Brantford, Ontario. This will be my first published work. I currently live in California, where I am pursuing a degree in Native social work.

Margot LeBrasseur: (Chippewa) I have been writing for three years, but this is the first time I've shared it with anyone. I work as a research assistant of Pennsylvania State College.

Bea Medicine: (Lakota) I was born in 1923 on the Standing Rock reservation. I am involved in political and ritual events, and was chosen the Sacred Pipe Woman in the revival of our Sun Dance in 1977. I am an anthropologist and have taught at many universities.

Terri Meyette: (Yaqui) I'm thirty, a lesbian, and a poet. I am currently incarcerated in Santa Maria prison in Goodyear, Arizona.

Mary Moran: I am a lesbian writer and artist, born and raised in the rural midwest. My mother is French-Canadian and Native American. My family denied the Native identity and my writing reflects an exploration of my search for a sense of who I am. I'm thirty-six and live in Los Angeles.

Nora Naranjo-Morse: (Santa Clara/Tewa) I presently live in Nambe, New Mexico, with my husband and my two children. I came from Santa Clara Pueblo thirty years ago and make my way through life writing and making pottery.

Nila NorthSun: (Shoshone/Chippewa) I'm thirty-one, live on my rez in Fallon, Nevada. Author of two books of poetry. I'm married, have two kids, like Mexican food, rum and cokes, gardening, and eating sweets.

Share Ouart: (Rosebud Sioux) I'm thirty years old, and a mother. I'm presently serving a term in Mable Bassett Correctional Center in Oklahoma City, Oklahoma.

Denise Panek: (White Earth Chippewa) I consider my poetry a gift. I have come full circle to where I belong and believe it is through the spiritual encouragement from those who lived before me. I live in Wisconsin.

Edith Purevich: (Chippewa/Eastern Shawnee) I am forty-nine years old, have four adult children. I live very quietly, with my poems, my books, and my cats, in Grandview, Missouri.

Lynn Randall: (Oglala) I was born in 1951. I live in Pine Ridge Village, South Dakota.

Raven: (Doris Ann Foster) (Cherokee) I am twenty-eight and love living free. I am serving a life term in Jessup, Maryland. I would like to correspond with my Indian sisters.

Marcie Rendon: (Ojibway) My name, Awanequay, translates as Fog-Woman. I'm thirty-one and belong to the Eagle Clan. I'm a lay midwife and mother of two daughters. I live in Minneapolis, Minnesota.

Diane Reyna: (Taos Pueblo) I have been a still photographer for ten years. I am completing my fourth year as a television news photographer with KOAT-TV in Santa Fe.

Wendy Rose: (Hopi/Miwok) I was born in 1948. Author of seven poetry books. Editor of *American Indian Quarterly*. I live in Leftovers, California (El Sobrante), with a magician and a middle-aged cat.

Alice Sadongei: (Kiowa/Papago) I'm twenty-three and have been writing since I was fourteen. I write about what is familiar, about being Indian. I live in Phoenix, Arizona.

Carol Lee Sanchez: (Laguna/Sioux/Lebanese) I'm forty-nine, a poet, painter, and playwright. I'm a mother of three children, and the author of two books of poetry.

Kateri Sardella: (Micmac) I am thirty, a lesbian, a writer of short stories and poems. I was born in upstate New York, and now live in California.

Doris Seale: (Santee/Cree) I'm forty-six and have been writing something or other for as long as I can remember. I sometimes think "half-breed" is a whole separate species; sometimes it feels that way. I live in Massachusetts.

Vickie Sears: (Cherokee) I'm forty, a lesbian, and have been writing since I was six. I live in Seattle, Washington, where I work as a feminist therapist.

Kate Shanley: (Assiniboine/Irish) I am thirty-five, born and raised on the Fort Peck reservation in Montana. I'm a single mother of a twelve-year-old son, and working on my Ph.D. in literature at the University of Michigan.

Rita Silk-Nauni: (Standing Rock Sioux) I'm presently serving a one-hundred-year sentence for manslaughter in Mable Bassett Correctional Center in Oklahoma City, Oklahoma.

Jaune Quick-To-See-Smith: (Flathead) Born in 1940 on the Flathead Reserve in Montana. Now lives in Corrales, New Mexico.

Alice Souligny: (Cherokee/Delaware) Born in 1931 in Oklahoma. I started painting in 1976. I am a mother and a grandmother. I believe that painting is a way of education. To pass knowledge to others.

Amber Coverdale Sumrall: (Mohawk) I'm thirty-seven and live in the Santa Cruz mountains, cozy inside my trailer, with seven cats. Writing is my way of processing and releasing deep feeling.

Midnight Sun: (Nishnawbe/Métis) I'm twenty-one, actively involved with Native groups in prison. Have always lived in the city (Toronto). Am a first-year student at York University, majoring in Native Studies. Trying to maintain some balance in a crazy world.

Debra Swallow: (Oglala) Born in 1954, went to school at Oglala Community College. I live in Manderson, South Dakota.

Mary TallMountain: (Koyukon) I am sixty-four years old, born in Alaska. My years have been packed with excitement and mucho love and inspiration, along with some or just enough sorrow to fill up the package.

Luci Tapahonso: (Navajo) Born in 1951, a mother, a writer. Currently living in Albuquerque, New Mexico.

Gayle Two Eagles: (Lakota) I am thirty, mother of two adopted children. I live in South Dakota, where I am attempting to finish college. All you closet Indian feminists, come out!

Anita Valerio: (Blood/Chicana) I am twenty-six, a lesbian. I feel as though my entire life I've been a renegade. I have had to re-invent myself in order to survive. I live in San Francisco, California.

Anna Lee Walters: (Pawnee/OtoeMissouri) I work at Navajo Community College in Tsaile, Arizona.

Elizabeth Woody: (Navajo) I'm twenty-three years old and have previously published in *Spawning the Medicine River*. I live in Santa Fe, New Mexico.

Jane A. Kresovich

Beth Brant (*Degonwadonti*) was born May 6, 1941. She is a Bay of Quinte Mohawk from Deseronto, Ontario. She has been writing since the age of forty and her work has appeared in numerous Native and feminist journals and anthologies in Canada and the U.S. She is the author of *Mohawk Trail*, a collection of prose and poetry published by Firebrand Books. Beth has twice been the recipient of the Michigan Council for the Arts Creative Artist award. She is the mother of three daughters and grandmother of two grandsons. She lives in Detroit with her partner of twelve years, Denise.

The cover art is by Charleen Touchette. "My art is inspired by my dreams, memories, and visions. The power of my matriarchal heritage ('Metis'—French Canadian and Indian) has given me the inner strength to walk in balance and dignity. I believe that the power of visionary art can contribute to a future where all Four Colors of the People can walk together in harmony on Mother Earth."

ALSO FROM WOMEN'S PRESS:

Enough Is Enough: Aboriginal Women Speak Out

A small group of women from a reserve called Tobique embarrassed the Canadian government in front of the world and brought the plight of Native women and Native experience to the eyes of millions.

These are their stories about growing up Native and female. It is the story of a struggle to end one hundred years of legislated sexual discrimination against Native women in Canada. Their struggle started with the occupation of a band office, continued with a hundred-mile march to Ottawa and ended up in the United Nations.

254 pages   6 x 9
$11.95 paperback   0-88961-101-7

Individuals may order directly from Women's Press, 229 College St., Toronto M5T 1R4. Please enclose full payment with your order adding postage and handling—$1.00 for the first book plus .50 for each additional book.

Not Vanishing
by Chrystos (published by Press Gang)

Not Vanishing is a remarkable first book of poetry by Native American lesbian poet, Chrystos. Well known for her contributions to the anthologies *This Bridge Called My Back* and *A Gathering Of Spirit*, Chrystos writes in a strong distinctive voice about racism in America, about self-esteem and survival.

120 pages   5 x 8
$9.50   0-88974-015-1

Individuals may order directly from Press Gang Publishers, 603 Powell St., Vancouver, B.C. V6A 1H2. Please enclose full payment with your order adding postage and handling—$2.00 for the first book, plus .50 for each additional book.

Your bookstore may also order these books through University of Toronto Press, 5201 Dufferin St., Downsview, Ontario M3H 5T8, (416) 667-7791, FAX (416) 667-7832.